Praise

"Great fun to read, ranges over l[...]
full of practical tips for people wh[...] ~~[...]~~ *or for those*
who work or live with them. So much more inspiring than typical time
management books and it adds a missing dimension to Stephen Covey's
work. And for me, the tips on how to use deadlines and manage
distractions are spot on!

CATHERINE STOTHART, LEADERSHIP COACH AND AUTHOR OF
"HOW TO GET ON WITH ANYONE"

"'LATE!' is an insightful and intriguing book. As well as a helpful
guide for partners and friends, this would also be a useful book for
managers to work more effectively with any Timebending staff! There
are plenty of practical tips to expand your leadership repertoire."

JOE CHEAL, AUTHOR OF "SOLVING IMPOSSIBLE PROBLEMS"
AND "WHO STOLE MY PIE?" AND OWNER OF IMAGINARIUM
LEARNING & DEVELOPMENT

"Everything you write is so true! I laughed out loud on many occasions!
It really is such a good antidote to all the other time management books
out there! I found it funny, informative, and sympathetic to other
people. The Demon Deadline Shaver, Always Keep an Untidy Desk
and being truthful about being late still live with me on a daily basis."

CLARE RAYNER, MFOM

"'Timebending'! What a relief to have someone label this and double
relief to know I am not alone! This is a must read for anyone who
desires a more harmonious life. As a parent and CEO, I related to so
much in this book and now have tips to not only make my own life less
stressful, but I can for those Timekeepers around me, too. This book
was far more insightful and thought provoking that I expected."

REBECCA JONES, CEO OBJECT SOURCE LLP

"I like the way it steers away from the conventional idea that it's just a 'lack of discipline.' I found the tips insightful, practical and easy to implement."

STEPHANIE REES, REGIONAL DIRECTOR, STRATEGY PLUS

"This subject is of interest to a wide market, yet there are very few books about it. It is well-researched with a solid scientific base."

DR. ALISON BAVERSTOCK, ASSOCIATE PROFESSOR OF PUBLISHING AT KINGSTON UNIVERSITY, AUTHOR OF "MARKETING YOUR BOOK," AND BOARD MEMBER OF THE SOCIETY OF AUTHORS

"After reading 'LATE!' I now better understand why I'm always in the car waiting for my husband and, more importantly, what to do about it! It's a fun, easy read with a lot of practical tips for people who have to live with someone who is chronically 'bending time.'"

JOY WODZIAK, STRATEGIC MARKETING CONSULTANT

"'LATE!' shows that effective time-management techniques for 'Perceiving' types tend to be nuanced and are not at all like traditional time management techniques. There is a lot of energy in this topic!

ANN C. HOLM, MS, PCC, CPCC, MBTI MASTER PRACTITIONER AND PROFESSIONAL CERTIFIED COACH

"As a journalist who has never missed a deadline, I grit my teeth over the habitually late who frankly baffle me. Why can't they do things or get to places on time? It's not rocket science after all. This entertaining and well-researched book helps me understand where they're coming from and helps them understand what stops them being timely and what to do about it. A fascinating read whether or not time is a problem for you."

WENDY BERLINER, AWARD-WINNING JOURNALIST AT THE GUARDIAN, AND CO-AUTHOR OF "GREAT MINDS AND HOW TO GROW THEM," AND "HOW TO SUCCEED AT SCHOOL: SEPARATING FACT FROM FICTION"

"A great book for someone who has just been struck with how their behavior impacts others and would like to keep their job, marriage or friendship, but without losing themselves. The Secret Scale of Acceptable Lateness is a very effective tool for comparing relative perceptions of timeliness."

STEPHEN MARTIN, HEAD OF EMEA,
FRANK LYNN & ASSOCIATES

"On a practical level, this book helps us understand our impact on friends and colleagues whose notion of 'late' may differ from ours. And it provides some excellent tools for improving our performance if, when, and where we choose. Although its main focus is on the ends of a continuum, this book is also extremely relevant to those of us somewhere in the middle. In a world where most people play multiple roles and interact with hundreds of people, 'LATE!' provides unique insights that promote mutual understanding on a dimension seldom discussed."

SUSAN HEINTZ, PRESIDENT, CHANNEL MANAGEMENT
PROFESSIONALS LLC; BOARD PRESIDENT
OF VISCERAL DANCE CHICAGO.

"'LATE!' explains the P preference so well, providing me with new insights and a much better understanding. It made a great impression on me, recognizing how I as an ENFP underestimate time, and get sidetracked by something that was not my goal. It provides great questions I can use personally for development but also as a typology practitioner. It was entertaining and thought provoking, giving me so many more layers of insight into the P behavior."

LISETTE TOWNSEND, STRATEGIST & MEDIATOR,
TOWNSEND CONSULTING

To Elena,

Thanks for all the
encouragement!

Grace Pacié

LATE!

A Timebender's Guide to Why We Are Late and How We Can Change

By Grace G. Pacie
Illustrated by Karen Tweed

Punchline Publications

ISBN: 978 1 8380705 1 9

Also available on Kindle
ISBN: 978 1 8380705 0 2

Web: www.timebending.co.uk
Facebook page: Not Late but Timebending
Facebook group: Not Late but Timebending group
Twitter: @OnlyTimebending

Cover design by Richard Moon

Published by Punchline Publications

Contents

PART ONE

Why Can't We Be on Time?

Welcome to Our Secret Society

"*I'm sorry I'm late but...*" How often do you say these words? And how often do you manage to arrive on time just because all the traffic lights were green and you found the perfect parking space? If this picture is familiar, then join the club – a surprisingly large club, which has been a secret society for far too long.

Let's face it – we hate being late! When we do arrive early, we enjoy feeling calm and unruffled, with enough time to visit the bathroom or get a cup of coffee. So why don't we make our lives easier by doing it all the time? We always make mental notes that *next time* we will leave home earlier, *next time* we won't break the speed limit trying to make up time, *next time* we won't embarrass ourselves by walking into an event after it has started. It's just that somehow, when it comes to the *next time,* our resolve evaporates and we fall back into the same pattern.

Do you get the feeling that the rest of the world is always on time, and it is just you who is always late? It's a surprisingly common problem – in 2014, a YouGov poll found that 19% of US workers are late for work at least once a week, and Joseph Ferrari, Professor of Psychology at DePaul University in Chicago, has established that 20% of people struggle with being on time. People are very quick to criticize our lack of punctuality, but if one in five of us is often late, what research has been carried out to help us understand and improve our behavior? We aren't like the 80% of the population who find it easy to be

3

punctual – time seems to work differently for us. Writers of Time Management courses and books haven't grasped that we need an alternative approach – they seem to think everyone can follow simple instructions to change their behavior. We need to creep up on the problem from a different angle if we are to find ways of arriving on time, because we have a little demon in our brain that is determined to make us late.

This book explores our singular relationship with punctuality because, if we can find ways of improving our timekeeping, we will be improving lives. Not just our own lives, but the lives of the people we live and work with. Close to every person who is always late, there will be someone who needs to be early, and the sparks that fly between the two could power a city. Unfortunately for them, the early birds get the worst of the bargain, though they play an important role in our lives. They act like a pressure gauge – the nearer they get to exploding, the faster we move. So in the interests of reducing global tensions, we need to see if we can find better ways of becoming our own time-keepers.

We can often be the last people to admit we have a problem. We always imagine that we're going to be on time, so it is easy to blame our lateness on the traffic, or the fact that we had to do something just before we left home. It is only when we take a deep breath, and recognize that it ALWAYS happens, that we can start to see the problem as something personal.

Although we'd all love to find a magic solution that will make us punctual, we know that's just a dream. We know from personal experience that there aren't any easy answers – it's very hard to change our behavior, because we've tried again and again. But if we can't find a way to simply reprogram our brains, there are other ways to address the issue, and in these pages you'll find some surprisingly simple and effective ideas to help you manage the problem.

This book starts by mapping out the mental mazes which result in us being late, because once we understand what triggers our behavior, we are halfway to the solution. Next, we open the Timebender's Toolbox, which is packed with practical tips and ideas to help you to be on time when it matters. After this we take a step back, to look at how our lateness patterns change at different points in our lives, where the special challenges lie, and how to deal with them. Once we have understood this broader perspective, we delve deeper into the subject, by looking into the neuroscience of what is happening in our brains, and whether therapy can help. Since many of the people reading this book will be looking for insights into how to live with someone who is always late, we offer advice about which strategies will help us to improve our timekeeping, and which are likely to have the opposite effect. Finally, we offer a selection of workbook exercises to help achieve long-term change.

So let's not waste any time. Let's start with a quick quiz, to show you where you fit on the lateness scale.

Time for a Quiz

1. When I'm not working at it, the surface of my desk:
   a) Is always completely clear

   b) Is sorted and tidy

   c) Is usually piled with papers

2. When I go to a regular activity or class:
   a) I always get there early (unless something exceptional happens)

   b) I aim to get there early, and usually arrive in good time

   c) I aim to arrive at the start time, but sometimes I'm late

3. If something unexpected happens to interrupt my work schedule:
   a) I like to be in control of my schedule and hate it to be disrupted

   b) I don't mind being flexible if it's something important

   c) I rather enjoy the distraction, and hope I can still catch up on my scheduled work

4. If I'm expecting a visitor, and they don't arrive on time:
   a) I get annoyed, as I think it's rude to be late

   b) I don't really mind if they're a bit late

   c) I'm pleased, because I manage to get lot done in those extra minutes

5. When doing domestic chores:
    a) I have a regular routine which I follow with little variation
    b) I generally follow the same routine, but can change this if necessary
    c) I don't have a regular routine

6. When working out how long it will take to do a job:
    a) I'm more likely to allow too much time
    b) I'm pretty accurate in estimating how long things take
    c) I sometimes find I haven't left enough time

7. When I go on vacation:
    a) My bag is packed several days beforehand, apart from toiletries etc.
    b) My bag is always packed and ready in good time on the day of departure
    c) I don't usually manage to close my bag until almost the last minute

8. When I'm doing a job or hobby which creates a mess:
    a) I really look forward to putting everything away again
    b) I normally clear up everything when I've finished
    c) I don't look forward to clearing up, and sometimes I put it off

9. If someone has offered to pick me up from home:
    a) I like to be ready and waiting by the door 10 minutes before they arrive, in case they are early
    b) I'm always completely ready by the time we agreed
    c) I'm often not quite ready, when they arrive to pick me up

10. If I'm given a job with a long deadline:
   a) I would get the job finished early, so it is out of the way
   b) I plan my work so that it is comfortably finished and checked by the deadline
   c) I am usually working hard, right up to the cut-off point

How Did You Score?

Mostly A's

o You get very irritated by people who are late, and can't understand why they don't fix the problem.

o You plan your time carefully, and can get obsessive about the need to be early.

o You are probably reading this book because you are finding it difficult to live with someone who is always late.

This book can help you to understand why people are late, and give you some strategies to help you manage the negative impact on your life.

Mostly B's

o You are well-organized and don't find it difficult to be on time.

o You would think it a waste of time to be early for everything.

o You can get frustrated with people who hold you up because they are late.

The majority of the population are like you. You struggle to understand the A's and C's in your life. This book will give you some perspective on other people's issues with punctuality, and allow you to appreciate your own easy relationship with time.

Mostly C's

- You don't enjoy being late, and would like to arrive on time ALL the time.
- Unless you have an important appointment, you rarely arrive early.
- You are late more often than you like to admit.
- You believe you get a lot more done at the last minute than people who are always early and waiting around, doing nothing.

This book will give you insights into your behavior, and equip you with practical ways to improve your relationship with time.

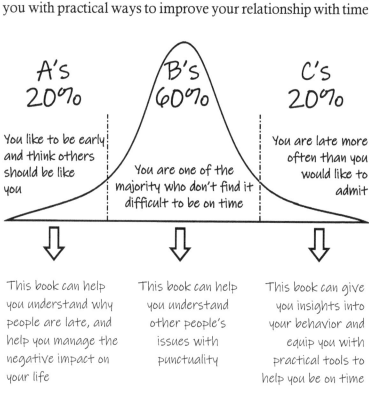

A's
20%

You like to be early and think others should be like you

B's
60%

You are one of the majority who don't find it difficult to be on time

C's
20%

You are late more often than you would like to admit

This book can help you understand why people are late, and help you manage the negative impact on your life

This book can help you understand other people's issues with punctuality

This book can give you insights into your behavior and equip you with practical tools to help you be on time

We all sit somewhere on the continuum, and we all have something to learn from each other. If you are fortunate enough to be one of the 60% majority who have an easy relationship with punctuality, this book will show you how it can be a problem for other people at both ends of the spectrum.

If you have a need to be early, it will help you understand why some people are late, and Part Five will give you some ideas for managing the impact of their behavior on your life.

If you are one of the 20% who struggle to be on time, this book is designed to help you. You will learn what triggers your lateness, and when it is likely to occur. Part Two is packed with tried and tested tools which can help you to be on time. This book is an attempt to explain a pattern of behavior which has remained hidden for too long, and to start a dialog which will hopefully result in a better understanding from all sides.

A Window on Our World

"I've been on a calendar, but I've never been on time."
MARILYN MONROE

When Maya meets up with her Poetry Slam team in San Francisco, Jake and Karl are always early, the rest of the gang are just on time, but Joey is usually 10 minutes late. When Li Qiang arrives at the local tea house for his weekly game of Mahjong, he usually finds that Liu Wei and Zhang Yong are there before him, but Li Jie always rushes in at the last minute. When Rob plays in a weekly match game at his golf club in the Cotswolds, Ian always arrives at least 30 minutes early, while Dave always rushes in seconds before the draw, and sometimes misses the match entirely.

Wherever you are in the world, the story is the same, with one in five people struggling to be on time, and an equal number anxiously needing to arrive early. So let's take a look at what lies behind this behavior.

Carl Jung was the first person to demonstrate that human nature isn't as random as it seems. He showed us that we have clear and predictable patterns, which are based on differences in our deep-seated preferences. One of the key differences he identified is that some of us prefer to get things closed down and finished, and others prefer to keep our options open. Or, to put it another way, some people always want to be early, and others have a tendency to be late. Jung's theories were turned into a personality indicator (known as MBTI) which has since been used to assess personality differences in over 50 million people around the world. (See Appendix.) The results show us that around half of us enjoy the feeling of getting things finished and the other half feel uncomfortable with closure. Most people sit somewhere in the middle, but about 20% of us lie at each end of the scale. The surprising truth is, you are late or early because you were born that way.

Since those in the middle don't have an issue with punctuality, we'll focus on the people at each end of the spectrum. As far as time is concerned, the world is divided into two different species, so it might help if we gave each a label… **Timekeepers** and **Timebenders**. We not only have different temperaments, but we usually have different friends, we are attracted to different types of jobs, we respond to different incentives, we get pleasure from different situations, and we are driven by different motives.

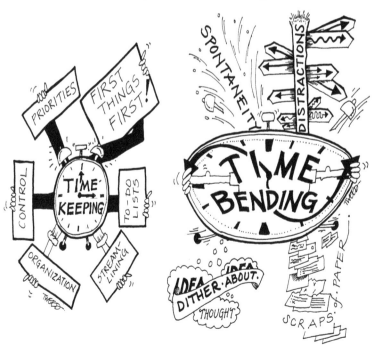

TIMEKEEPERS	TIMEBENDERS
Are usually earliest to arrive	Are usually last to arrive
Like to finish tasks ahead of time	Very rarely finish tasks ahead of time
Get annoyed when events don't start on time	Don't see why other people get so bothered about starting on time.
Feel uncomfortable if the time available for a task is squeezed	Get energized by tight time-scales
Work at a constant pace	Can speed up if time is short
Are good at measuring how long a task will take	Can be unrealistic in estimating the time needed for a task
Can't think too clearly when they have to get something finished in a hurry	Can focus well when they are being squeezed by a tight deadline
Love finishing tasks	Put off finishing things
Are usually thinking about their next activity before they have finished their current task	Tend to linger in the moment and can be reluctant to shut down what they are doing
Like a clear desktop	Usually have piles of papers on their desks
Do not like being interrupted	Don't mind being distracted
Are likely to refuse, when asked to take on extra work within a set deadline	Hesitate to turn away something that interests them, even if time is short

The day-to-day life of a Timebender is surprisingly unpredictable. We can start the day with a clear idea of something we want to do – let's say send off a report, or get the car washed – but can end the day finding the job not yet finished. Terri is a typical case – she works long hours, and crams a lot into her weekends when she's at her home in St Albans. This is a fascinating insight into her life:

o *Last Saturday, while eating my breakfast, an hour before I had to leave for my exercise class, I noticed through the window that some leaves had piled up by the back door, so I decided to go and sweep them up.*

o *I had some mail I wanted to open, but it could wait, as it was a lovely autumn morning. On my way outside I saw the kitchen garbage was full, so I pulled out the bag and took it out.*

o *While throwing away the garbage I saw that some of my plant pots were dry, so I went off to the shed to get the watering can.*

o *When I opened the shed, I saw the bag of bird seed, which reminded me that I needed to refill the seeds in the bird feeder. As I did so, I waved to my neighbor next door, who was hanging out her laundry, and remembered that my laundry was ready, too.*

o *On the way back through the kitchen I put in a new garbage can liner and collected the laundry from the machine.*

o *As I was finishing hanging out the sheets, I noticed that the shed door was open, saw the watering can, and went to water the plant pots.*

o *On my way, I saw the leaves and remembered that I was going to sweep them up, but I realized I had run out of time. I quickly watered the pots, grabbed the brush from the shed, scooped up the leaves, put away the brush, rushed back inside, grabbed my gear and rushed out to my car, only three minutes late for my exercise class!*

A Timekeeper would judge this as a failure – the job in hand was not completed in time, and Terri was late for her class. A Timekeeper would have approached the morning very differently. They would have created a list of tasks and enjoyed working through them – reading the mail, filing the papers etc. They

would have allowed plenty of time to get ready for the class, arrived ten minutes early, and felt extremely comfortable and in control. Because they would have allowed a sensible amount of time for each job, they would have taken longer, but they would have felt really satisfied when they had finally finished the list.

From a Timebending perspective, arriving early would have been a terrible waste of time. Look at all the extra things that Terri achieved, and the deadline only missed by three minutes! To a Timebender, this is success!

Before this starts sounding too positive, there's another side to the picture. On a day when she had all morning to sweep the leaves, Terri might first have sat down to read the paper and still be in her pajamas by lunchtime.

So what's going on?

Who Wants to Eat Worms?

"I'm always late on principle, my principle being that
punctuality is the thief of time."

OSCAR WILDE

The problem is, deep down, Timebenders can't bear to be early. Being late is exciting – being early is boring. We can try to explain this logically – why would we want to be early for a doctor's appointment, and sit in a germ-filled waiting room reading outdated magazines? But the real reason is we'd rather be tearing around the house in an adrenaline rush, doing tasks that appear to be vitally important, just before we leave. Subconsciously we have convinced ourselves that those empty minutes spent waiting for something to begin are a complete waste of time, even though when we HAVE occasionally been early (probably by mistake), we might find ourselves chatting to someone interesting; or reading something useful on a notice board. Our minds aren't attracted to the idea of being early, just as Timekeepers have a deep aversion to being late. No matter how much we want to change this behavior, our unconscious minds make the decision and there's nothing we seem to be able to do about it.

At the other end of the scale, Timekeepers are the exact opposite. Their motto is: *"Early is on time, on time is late, and late is unacceptable."* Some people can be so averse to being late that even the thought of arriving on time fills them with fear, as Katie Sarott explains in Chicago Now: *"I am ALWAYS EARLY to appointments, meetings, events, dinners, dates, everything. I get really bad anxiety if I know I will be arriving right at the time I am supposed to meet someone (or, God forbid, after)."*

There is a subconscious reason underlying this anxiety. Extreme Timekeepers are secretly afraid something might go terribly wrong, so they allow extra time to deal with disasters. Jenni Maier confesses in The Muse: *"People who are always early tend to plan for every worst-case scenario – plus some that usually seem more well-suited to a horror movie. When I was interviewing for jobs earlier this year, I'd allot 15 minutes for a subway delay, and 10 minutes for running to Staples to print out my resume in case someone pushed me on the tracks and I had to choose between saving my life and saving my resume binder."*

Timekeepers tend to be looking ahead to what comes next, which can stop them from enjoying being in the moment, as Jerry explains *"I describe myself as time-bound. This is a curse. I am always checking my watch or a clock – everything is related to making use of time."* With one eye firmly fixed on the clock, they will be the ones who stop the fun and hurry everyone up. Abigail Taylor is a college student, which shows that this doesn't depend on age: *"The way some students keep to time, and keep their friends on time, comes across as a strict general trying to keep troops in line."*

Juno DeMelo, writing in the New York Times, describes the downside of wanting to get everything done as soon as possible: *"I flip pancakes before bubbles have formed on the surface; I get to the grocery store before it opens,"* she laments. She even remembers pulling out her milk teeth as soon as they were wobbly – ouch! This behavior can be so pronounced that David Rosenbaum, Psychology Professor at Pennsylvania State University, has even found a word for it – he has christened this behavior "Precrastination." Precrastinators are people who prefer to tackle tasks at the earliest opportunity — even if it takes them more effort. This term was adopted by Dr. Adam Grant, Professor of Management and Psychology at Wharton Business School in Pennsylvania, who described it as *"a perversion of diligence"*: *"What happens when you precrastinate is that your anxiety about making progress causes you to dive in headfirst, as opposed to giving yourself time to consider your options."*

Since its discovery in 2014, Precrastination has been found to exist in animals as well as humans, which has led Prof. Rosenbaum to consider the question of evolutionary advantage. He concludes that there are two benefits to being ahead of the pack – the "early bird" gets all the best food, and doesn't spend too much brainpower remembering "what to do when." He doesn't go on to point out the obvious risks to those who are always catching up the rear, where predators are on the lookout for easy prey.

There is a similar analogy used to describe competitive positions in business strategy, where the two camps are labelled Pioneers and Late Arrivals. In the business world, advantages can be seen on both sides – the Pioneers typically hold the lion's share of the market, but the Late Arrivals are able to exploit weaknesses and find new market opportunities without being exposed to the same amount of risk.

So let's consider the advantages in everyday life. Timekeepers get to enjoy the best of what's on offer – equipment at the gym, theatre seats, products in the shops etc., whereas Timebenders can sometimes pick up the cheapest bargains. From this viewpoint, it seems obvious we should all be motivated to be early. If only it was that simple.

One of the most powerful motives for a Timebender to give up their lateness habit should perhaps come from understanding the impact their behavior can have on others, and the distress they may be causing to friends or family members who suffer from paralyzing anxieties about being late. Knowing that they are going to meet someone who has been so worried about being late that they will have arrived 30 minutes early might help them to realize the importance of arriving on time.

So why don't Timebenders appear to be able to change their behavior, when it doesn't seem to have any benefits for them? What is stopping us from being early?

Don't Close that Door!

*"I stay up late every night, and realize it is a bad idea
every morning."*

ANON

Have you ever found that, just before you leave home, you
suddenly decide to go back and change your shoes? Or
just when you were off to bed, you had a compelling desire to
finish reading the paper? It seems quite normal to us at the
time, but if we look back on it, we can find that the things we
decide we absolutely MUST do, just before we leave, are not
actually as important as we convince ourselves they are. Opening the mail; watering the plants; wiping down the kitchen sink
– they can all be done just as well when we get home again.

As Jung showed us, Timekeepers can't wait to get things finished and put away, but Timebenders find it hard to reach that
moment of closure. It's a relief when we complete a task, but
we tend to have this nagging feeling that there is just one more
thing we need to do before we shut the door and leave; one
more piece of information we need to find before we finish our
report; one more program we need to watch before we go to
bed.

It comes from deep inside our subconscious – Timebenders
just don't feel comfortable with shutting things down. We like
to keep our options open, which can make us indecisive, and is
often the reason why we are late – just as we are rushing out the
door, we decide to go back and check whether we have turned

off the iron, or shut the bathroom window. The finality of locking suitcases and finishing essays gives us a hidden pang of anxiety which we would rather avoid. This is why we will keep adjusting reports until the very last minute, and adding items to our packed suitcases right until the taxi arrives.

Jane is married to an extreme Timebender and will never forget the day of her son's christening. The baby was washed and changed, her husband, Murphy was in his best suit and tie, and she was dressed up in her heels and hat, ready to get to the church half an hour early to meet the guests. *"I couldn't believe it. Just when we were all ready to leave, he decided this was the perfect time to fix the new cat door. He actually did the job dressed in his best clothes, and kept us all waiting. All our friends thought he was crazy."*

This type of behavior happens in every walk of life. Bill Clinton was famous for making last-minute cut-and-paste changes to all his major speeches, to the despair of White House officials. Nick, a highly paid consultant who flies around the world to

client meetings, continues tweaking his reports right until the moment his plane prepares for landing, regardless of the length of project. Academics and researchers can find it incredibly difficult to finish their books. Leila Salisbury, Director of University Press of Kentucky, has waited patiently for 30 years to publish a reference manual on amphibians and reptiles. Every time the publication seemed imminent, the author, who has spent three decades collecting data for the book, discovers a new data point, such as a new span of territory that a lizard inhabits. To Leila's frustration and despair, he can never manage to write the last word.

If we are extreme Timebenders, we can even find that we start to slow down as the deadline gets near. Once we see there are only five minutes to go, we get nervous of crossing the finishing line. When we look at the time and realize we have almost hit the deadline, we can go into slow motion. Deep down, we don't want to reach the end. My friend Betty is the most extreme Timebender I've ever met. I love her dearly, but her behavior can drive me crazy. For example, when I leave her house and she comes to the door to wave me off, she suddenly comes up with five things she hasn't asked me during our weekend together. As I'm driving away, I often have to stop and roll down the window, because she has one more thing she wants to say – she just doesn't want to let me go. She's the same on the telephone – she can never finish a conversation because she finds it impossible to say goodbye. She's just very uncomfortable with closure.

And sadly, closure isn't the only thing we don't like.

Can I Take Your Order?

*"I have always been a quarter of an hour before my time,
and it has made a man of me."*

HORATIO, LORD NELSON

When Carl Jung identified our deep-seated preferences, he identified a second important aspect to our behavior. While the Timekeeping half of the population likes to live a planned and organized life, and is happy to conform, the other (Timebending) half likes the flexibility to explore alternative options and new ideas, and dislikes routines and authority. Let's face it, we hate being ordered around, and can get surprisingly uncooperative if we're tied down. We need to be free to make our own choices, or the rebellious teenager inside our heads starts to get restless. So if you want to get a Timebender to cooperate, take care not to be too direct, because we really don't like being told what we must do, or how we must do it.

Debra found this to her cost, when she needed her husband to put his classic motorbike up for sale. She and Ben had agreed that they needed money to renovate their house, and the bike was an asset they could turn into cash. She often found Ben frustratingly disorganized, so she thought she would help him to focus. The first step was to remove the dust and grime that had accumulated during the bike's many years in their basement. She pinpointed the next free day that Ben would be able to tackle the job, got his agreement with the idea, and was pleased to see he was getting ready to start work before she left for the day.

When she came home, she had a shock – every tool and piece of equipment in their garage was clean and sparkling, but the classic bike hadn't been touched. Ben was unrepentant. *"I'm just getting around to it,"* he told her. Ben hadn't consciously decided not to work on the bike – he had just been distracted by other less important tasks. When we have a major project – something we MUST DO – we start to feel hemmed in and look around for ways of escape. This causes great frustration to Timekeepers, who work in a linear way, and carry out their tasks in a logical order, starting from the top. It can be one of the major causes of friction between us, because it appears that we are deliberately being uncooperative.

Linda is a Timekeeper married to a Timebender who wasn't very keen on getting down to routine maintenance tasks in their home. In fact, George took so long to get around to them, that she helpfully wrote them down on a list and taped them to the refrigerator. It took her some time to realize that, once a task was on the list, she could be certain it would NEVER get done. The list was brown and curled before she took it down rather wistfully, realizing that she needed to get a handyman in to finish the tasks, or do them herself.

But this doesn't mean that Timebenders will never do routine tasks. On the contrary, we will do them quite happily when we feel motivated. As we saw, Ben did a great job cleaning all the tools in the basement, but only because he should have been doing something else. We live in an upside-down world – we do our jobs the wrong way around.

Our Topsy-Turvy World

"The early bird gets the worm, but the second mouse gets the cheese."

STEVE WRIGHT, COMEDIAN

Timebenders are a contrary lot – whatever we should be doing, we want to do something else. Fortunately, other people aren't aware of this. If they knew, they would probably conclude that we are out of control and totally nuts. Every Timebender fears that this might be the horrible truth – but don't despair, because there is a hidden benefit to our craziness.

It's amazing what activities seem totally compelling when there's something daunting that we are avoiding. Architect Theo explained his struggles with his studies: *"When I was asked to write a 2,000-word history essay for my architecture degree, I waited to the last week to act. I decided to set all my other tasks aside so I could wholly focus on the essay. I locked myself in my room, and yet for the first six days I only wrote 100 words each day. My piano and guitar improved loads, and I saw lots of good movies, but this was not what I had been planning. It was only when the stress of a deadline and the possible retake of the module reached breaking point on the last day that I managed to complete the last 1,400 words."*

These days, our distractions are far less productive – social media, online games and "Breaking News" are lying in wait wherever we can lay our hands on a screen. Wasting time seems normal, because everybody does it – but is it? Ian has never forgotten how illogical some people can get: *"My friend*

Dave would do anything to avoid exam revision. At one point he infamously found himself weighing the cat, convinced that he would only be able to settle down to work if he had that piece of data. As a result, some 25 years later, the act of procrastination is referred to by my family as weighing the cat." This is a great example of how irrational we can get when we are avoiding our "must do" tasks.

But this contrariness can be a surprising source of energy, once we learn how to use it. We can get totally fascinated by things we aren't supposed to be doing – no matter how tedious they would normally seem. If we're trying to work at the kitchen table, we'll be wiping down the surfaces and cleaning the sink. If our workstation is in the bedroom, we'll be bleeding the radiator or reorganizing the closet. If we're working in the garage, we'll be sharpening chisels and cleaning paintbrushes. Beware of trying to do your work outside in the garden on a nice day, because you will have to deadhead every flower and kill every weed. Only when we're right up against that deadline will we finally turn to the big task we've been avoiding. This can be why Timebenders can sometimes be accused of being passive-aggressive – we will do things our own way and in our own time. Our partners can see our behavior as stubborn, though this isn't how it appears to us.

Megan McArdle, writing in the Atlantic Magazine, revealed how *"a talented and fairly famous colleague"* managed to regularly produce such highly-regarded 8,000-word features. He told her, *"Well, first, I put it off for two or three weeks. Then I sit down to write. That's when I get up and go clean the garage. After that, I go upstairs, and then I come back downstairs and complain to my wife for a couple of hours. Finally, but only after a couple more days have passed and I'm really freaking out about missing my deadline, I ultimately sit down and write."*

Bestselling author and guru Stephen Covey taught a generation of business people how to succeed, in his acclaimed book

"The 7 Habits of Highly Effective People." His golden rule advises everyone to divide their activities into four quadrants:

1. Important and urgent
2. Important and not urgent
3. Not important and urgent
4. Not important and not urgent

Timebenders turn this on its head – we start at number 4, and don't get to the important and urgent until we have no choice. Maybe this is why we're less likely to be captains of industry, but plenty of us are successful in other ways – as we will see later.

The fact that Timebenders never want to do what they SHOULD be doing has been proven in an academic study. Prof. Joseph Ferrari and Dianne Tice, working at De Paul University in Chicago in 2000, brought a group of students into a

lab and told them they were going to be asked to do a math puzzle, but there would be a delay beforehand. Half the students were told that the math puzzle was a serious test, and the other half were told that it would just be a bit of fun. While they were waiting, they had the option of practicing their math, or playing computer games. The students with Timebending tendencies who believed it was a serious test ALL played computer games.

Our crazy behavior is a boon to humorists. Keith Waterhouse tells the tale of a struggling freelance writer who wins a highly paid commission for a magazine article. The deadline comes and goes and the piece is never delivered. A further deadline – and still no article. Finally the editor dispatches an exasperated email: *"Either send the article urgently today or forget it."* To which he gets the reply *"I'm beginning the article as soon as I've finished cleaning my tennis shoes."*

So how do Timebenders manage to get through life with some semblance of order? Maybe writing a To Do list would be the answer?

To Do or Not to Do?

"I was expecting this, but not so soon."
TOMBSTONE INSCRIPTION, BOOT HILL, ARIZONA

There's no question about it – Timekeepers love To Do lists. They like to work to a schedule, and get deep satisfaction from ticking jobs off when they are finished. They have a good idea of how long each task will take, and may even tackle the items in priority order. They love the feeling of closure, as Jerry explains: *"I make lists and more lists and then I feel good when I scratch something off as DONE! ... To me everything on my list is important."* Timebenders have a different response. We like to write tasks down as a reminder to get them done, but we keep our lists informal, because we value spontaneity. As Sandy explains: *"I very much like to go with the flow, doing tasks as they appeal to me. I only make lists when I have to remember something."* We are more likely to scribble things down on the back of an envelope, and start a new list before we've finished the last one.

One very good reason why Timebenders are wary of lists is because they show us just how much there is to get done. We hate being bored, and as a result we often take on too much. As Jacky explains: *"I am notorious for filling my plate way too full, because I try to do everything, and I always plan way more than can possibly fit in a day. For this reason I am almost always 10-15 minutes late."*

Tony discovered the danger of writing lists in his busy job as Marketing Director of a British newspaper. He was always

31

"spinning plates," in a job that only a Timebender could do. The atmosphere was always crazy: each day was packed with one interruption after another, and it wasn't until the office was quiet at the end of the day that he could find a moment to think through his priorities and get the really important ones finished. This system worked well for Tony – he got a real buzz from his job, and his boss was happy, but his wife understandably wasn't. Tony felt under pressure to organize his time better, and one memorable day he sat down at his desk and wrote down all the things he needed to do. As the list got longer and longer, Tony found himself becoming more and more stressed. How could he possibly get it all done? It wasn't humanly possible. His pulse raced, his breathing got shallower and he had to slip outside for a walk to bring his stress levels under control. The moral of the story was clear to him – he could get his job done, as long as he didn't realize how much he had to do. Writing a list was disastrous, and he never tried it again. Tony soon recovered and kept his job, but as you might have guessed, he didn't keep his marriage.

Fortunately, there is another tool which Timebenders find fantastically helpful.

Pile on the Pressure!

"If it weren't for the last minute, nothing would ever get done."

There is one simple tool which turns Timebenders from timewasters into the most productive people on the planet! Give us a deadline and we can achieve miracles. We can do jobs in a fraction of the time it would take a Timekeeper. Our attention becomes focused and nothing distracts us from our task.

Catherine Lux managed to write her twelve-thousand-word Sociology and Communications dissertation at Brunel University in just 16 hours. *"I work really well under pressure. I'm a pretty fast writer once I have an idea in my head, but I really struggle when I have a lot of time to do something. I actually thought I would fail. My friends at Uni thought I was crazy. When I got a 2:1 I was sort of shocked, but also sort of not, because every essay I wrote at the last minute had pretty good grades."*

Catherine's marathon was exceptional, but every true Timebender knows they can get 80% of the job done in 20% of the time when a deadline is looming. Only last week I amazed even myself – 30 minutes before leaving for a committee meeting, I finally got around to checking the previous meeting minutes (which I had been meaning to check first thing that morning) and discovered that the whole purpose of the meeting was to review a detailed instruction sheet that I was supposed to have written! In just over half an hour I threw together four pages which would normally have taken me all day. (OK, you're right – I did arrive five minutes late.)

No Timekeeper can ever know what this astonishing power feels like. We believe we can work miracles. We become completely focused, and nothing gets in our way. We ignore all distractions. Our brain is firing on all cylinders and our fingers feel like they've doubled in number. It's an incredible power rush – though we never stop to enjoy the feeling, because we haven't a moment to spare. As the deadline approaches we can spot shortcuts, and make last minute changes to our plans, to speed things up. Our goal is the finishing line, and we will do anything to reach it. Elaborate details and additional flourishes go flying out the window – we just stick to what really matters. We don't tidy up as we go along – we leave the mess for later – or for somebody else.

The experience for Timekeepers is totally the opposite – they divide their time and their effort into equal slices. They don't have the Timebender's accelerator pedal – they work at a constant pace and get though their tasks in a calm and controlled manner. You might think that this means they would do a better job, but you'd be wrong, because they are driven by an opposite but equal need – they can't wait to get the job completed and out of the way. When Timekeepers can see the end in sight, they can't resist closing things down, even if there is more they could add. So they, too, will finish with the feeling that, if they'd spent more time, they could have improved their work.

Deadlines are an amazing tool for us, but they must adhere to two rules – they must be real and have consequences. The original term "deadline" had extremely serious repercussions – if you ignored it, you would die. The term comes from the American Civil War, where the "dead line" was a rough board fence, erected 20 feet inside the walls of a stockade in which

Federal prisoners were held captive. The guards on duty were instructed to *"shoot any prisoner who touches the dead line."* A real deadline is immovable and has serious ramifications. In other words, you can't make it up. A deadline that is plucked out of the air has as little effect as the sternly wagging finger, as author Douglas Adams knew when he famously said: *"I love deadlines. I love the whooshing sound they make as they fly by!"* If deadlines don't have dire consequences, they have no effect on us whatsoever. We're very hard to fool. We need that icy grip in the stomach which tells us that THIS TIME IT'S SERIOUS!!! We can't even ask other people to make up deadlines for us. Nothing will do, it seems, other than the threat of public humiliation, significant loss, serious injury – or death!

Bruce Springsteen and Paul McCartney were once famously stopped in their tracks by the consequences of a deadline. In July 2012, at a massive open-air concert in London's Hyde Park, they were having such a great time playing together at the finale that they didn't want to stop, and the audience didn't want them to stop either. But it hit the national news that they were switched off in mid-session, at 10:30pm precisely – the local noise curfew was more important than both of them.

Once we understand the need for consequences, we can recognize the stuff we're never going to get around to doing. You'll never bother making New Year Resolutions again. You know the sort I mean, *"I will join a gym and go regularly each week, I will clean the house every Saturday morning, and pay all my bills on time."* We don't even manage to achieve them in the first week, let alone the whole year. Timekeepers love them, but they just don't work for Timebenders.

This explains why so many Timebenders were surprised to find that, at the end of the Coronavirus lockdown, they hadn't managed to complete a fraction of the jobs they had promised themselves they would tackle. Timekeepers made full use of this opportunity, and many of them managed to tick off all the tasks on their list. Timebenders were missing one vital element in the mix – there was no predictable deadline. If the course of the virus could have been foreseen, then Timebenders could have finished lockdown with a flurry of activity. Instead, most looked back with amazement at how much time they had spent getting distracted by social media and other unproductive pastimes. Not everyone's task list involved painting the fence or tiling the bathroom – many artists, photographers and writers had creative projects they had hoped to finish during lockdown, without success. Creativity and lateness very often go hand in hand, because Timebenders are constantly seeing new potentialities – which is why we need a real external deadline to fall like a guillotine and cut off our unlimited ideas. This makes life extremely difficult for executives who need to get writers to finish their manuscripts in advance of the final deadline.

Aaron Sorkin, the acclaimed screenwriter behind "Steve Jobs" and "The West Wing," is known for putting off writing until the last minute. Spike Milligan, another creative genius, caused the BBC serious trouble by never submitting his script in good time, as a letter preserved in their archives confirms:

Dear Mr. Milligan,

It has been reported to me by Mr. Peter Eton that, despite his constant requests for early delivery, your scripts continue to arrive late, in some cases not until the morning of the prerecording.

Douglas Adams' publisher at Pan Books, Sonny Mehta, had so much experience of dragging authors kicking and screaming over the finishing line that he knew exactly what to do to get Douglas to finish the sequel to his hugely successful masterpiece "Hitchhiker's Guide to the Galaxy." The follow-up was several years late, and a lot of money was riding on global contracts.

Sonny Mehta knew he had to make the deadline real and non-negotiable. He hired a suite at The Berkeley and moved in with Douglas until he had finished his manuscript. No wriggling out, no "tidying the cupboard under the sink" – this was serious. Not only was the hotel suite costing a fortune, but a very senior executive was suspending his own business activities for weeks. The double whammy of public humiliation and huge expense finally did the trick for Douglas, and he finished his book.

You have to feel sorry for anyone who needs to motivate a Timebender. Douglas Adams knew that he had a problem, but most of us are not so self-aware – we always think that next time we won't be late. What is going on in our heads?

Beware the Demon Deadline Shaver

"Better to Arrive Late than be Dead on Time."
ROAD SAFETY SIGN, WARIMOO ROAD, AUSTRALIA

How can one half of our brain always want to be on time, but somehow get over-ruled by the other half? Whenever we plan to be early, we seem to have an inner demon who keeps on shaving off those extra minutes we built in, until we are right down to the wire.

In our minds, we always plan to be punctual. *"If I set the alarm for 7am, I'll have plenty of time to get ready, and can leave the house 10 minutes early."* It sounds perfectly possible for life to be calm and predictable. But it also sounds horribly boring to our inner saboteur, who loves to keep us on the edge, right down to the last minute – and beyond.

The problem is that this inner demon is in control of the adrenaline switch in our brain. That's the moment when we yell *"Oh sh*t! Is that the time!"* and leap into action. Our demon decides when to switch on the panic button, makes up its own mind about what is the real deadline, and *only keeps a record of the shortest time we have ever taken.* This little demon overrules anything our common sense is telling us.

Once you start to recognize your Demon Deadline Shaver, you can spot him at his work. For example, if I make a conscious decision that I want to get to my exercise class in good time, and decide I will allow 20 minutes for the drive and 10 minutes to get into the building and chat to friends, he sits on my shoulder and drops distractions in my path, until I find that somehow I am leaving home only 15 minutes before the class starts – which was the time I once managed to get there when all the traffic lights were green and the roads were empty.

This explains why we can be early when we go somewhere for the first time. We haven't given our demon a chance to start using his stopwatch. The problem occurs when we have a regular and predictable journey, as we will arrive later and later, because we keep shaving down the moment when we leave home. It also explains the reason why the people who live closest to a meeting location are often the last to arrive, as their journeys are the most predictable. And it isn't just the journey, it all starts with the first deadline – the time when we have to start getting ready. If we think we're going to leave the house at 8:30am, will we allow the half hour it take us to get to that point? Needless to say, if we once managed to get ready in 20 minutes, our Demon Deadline Shaver will only hit the panic button as 8:10am approaches, which means that we will always miss breakfast.

When satellite navigation was introduced into cars in the 1990s, it seemed to be a gift to Timebenders, as it told us the time a car journey would take before we set off – so why would we ever be late again? We were slow to notice our Demon Deadline Shaver rubbing his hands with glee at all the fun he was going to have. We now find him sharing our driving seat, pushing us to break the speed limit, because no matter how hard we try, it's virtually impossible for a true Timebender not to set off five minutes late. Our Demon feeds on adrenaline, and there is nothing he enjoys more than the white-knuckle ride, as we race to make up time on the journey.

Timekeepers don't understand why we can't see the problem.

They have never come across the Demon Deadline Shaver. The solution seems so obvious to them – get up earlier, get ready faster and just leave home earlier. If only it was that easy!

THE DEMON DEADLINE SHAVER

Our Demon also has another trick up his sleeve – he completely blanks out "transition time" – the time it takes us to get ready. Mine just shuts his eyes and sticks his fingers in his ears and shouts *"La, la, la lah!"* while I pack my bag, put on my coat, go back upstairs to find my phone, collect a bottle of water from the fridge, search for my keys, feed the cat, leave the house and lock the door, walk into the garage and start the engine. This usually takes me around 10 minutes, but I never seem to factor this in.

Clare lives in an apartment complex and parks her car in the basement under the building. As a Timebender, she is always late for work. One day she managed to measure the time it took to get from her front door to her car, and was amazed to find it took seven whole minutes – she would have guessed one or two minutes. *"I couldn't believe it took me so long,"* she told me. *"But I*

41

still can't seem to allow for those seven minutes when I'm getting ready. No wonder I'm always late for work!"

Transition time disappeared for a few miraculous weeks during the COVID-19 lockdown, when meetings and classes were run online, and all we needed to do was log in. Finally, we had found our dream scenario – we could teleport ourselves instantly to where we needed to be, at the exact start time! Timekeepers, on the other hand, would be sitting patiently waiting for the host to open the meeting, comfortable and in control, ten minutes before it was due to begin.

It's easy to blame our Demon Deadline Shaver for making us late, but maybe we have another handicap?

It's About Time

"When a man sits with a pretty girl for two hours, it seems like two minutes. But let him sit on a hot stove for two minutes – then it seems like two hours. That's relativity!"

ALBERT EINSTEIN

Timebenders are at a big disadvantage – we don't really know how long anything takes. One day we can take all morning to get dressed, because we have no deadline and keep getting distracted, and the next day it can take us only ten minutes, because we are in a rush. As a result, when we try to work out how much time to allow for getting dressed, we just take a wild guess.

Experiments have shown that people who are late are poor at measuring time. A 2001 study by Jeff Conte, an associate psychology professor at San Diego State University, claimed that people who are always late have a "Type B" personality, and went on to demonstrate that they perceive time differently. "Type A" individuals are described as fast-paced, achievement-oriented and sometimes hostile, whereas "Type B" individuals are more laid back.

In his simple but revealing experiment, Jeff asked people to measure how long they thought a minute was, without looking at a clock. "Type A" averaged guesses of 58 seconds, whereas "Type B" averaged 77 seconds. This means that, for every minute of the day, "Type B" people seemingly believe they have an extra 17 seconds, so it comes as no surprise that they're late.

Diana DeLonzor conducted a similar experiment at San Francisco State University, where she compared the time-measuring ability of a sample of people who were always late with a control group. She asked them to read some pages of a book and stop when they thought 90 seconds had elapsed. "I

TIME KEEPER

TIME BENDER

found that early birds, almost without fail, stopped reading before nine-ty seconds had passed, while late people put their books down well after the ninety-second mark," she said.

Not only do these experiments show that Timebenders aren't good at measuring time, but it also shows that Timekeepers are pretty good at it. This is an important clue to the differences between us. Timekeepers can easily estimate how long it takes to complete a task, because they see time as linear, not flexible. An administrator knows how long it will take to process a form. An engineer can calculate how much time is needed to assemble a set of parts. An inspector can assess how much time is needed to carry out an audit. For these people, a task always takes the same amount of time, and a tight deadline makes them feel un-comfortable and interferes with their concentration. Their atti-tude to time is totally different.

> *"I hate it when my boss asks me to get my work done in a hurry. It's really counter-productive. I find I just slow down, and sometimes make mistakes, because the pres-sure distracts me."*
>
> DEBORAH WINN, BOOKKEEPER

Timekeepers will often plan their day by writing a list of things they have to do, and have a clear idea how much time to allow for each activity:

- o Get up – 1 min
- o Shower – 12 minutes
- o Get dressed – 13 minutes
- o Eat breakfast – 11 minutes
- o Clean teeth – 2 minutes
- o etc.

46

Timebenders would be so bored with this plan that we wouldn't bother to get out of bed! Our day is full of interesting little twists and turns, diversions and dead ends, interrupted by a few hectic races to the finish line. Since we tackle our jobs the wrong way around, whenever we know we HAVE TO get something done, we immediately think of doing something else. How on earth do we know how long any of it takes? As Hal explains: "*I have difficulty estimating the time it will take to accomplish something. This is probably due to the fact I don't see all the steps clearly. It also has to do with motivation: if I want to do it, the time doesn't matter; if not, all the time in the world wouldn't be enough.*"

We know that our mental state makes a real difference to how quickly we finish a task. When we aren't motivated, we can spend all day dithering. However, when the chips are down, and we have a tight and immoveable deadline, we can achieve amazing results.

The closer we get to the deadline, the faster we believe we can move. It seems ridiculous, but when I am rushing to get ready, I can honestly imagine that I will be able to clean my teeth, get washed and dressed, feed the cat, put on my shoes and jacket, sort out my bag, open and lock the door and get into the car in 20 minutes flat. It is only when my electric toothbrush starts to slowly measure the two minutes I always take to clean my teeth that I realize how magical this thinking is.

Rhoda is a Timekeeping mum who noticed this problem on the school run: *"I talked to my friend who always gets her kids to school late, and realized she genuinely has a mental block about factoring in how long things take – so if she was leaving home at 8:55 and it was a 10 minute walk to school, she would still think she was on time, until the clock literally ticked past nine o'clock."*

ML has an interesting insight into what might be going on: *"Rather than being in denial about how time works, I think I lack some kind of 'time depth perception.' Like if you don't have bifocal vision, you wouldn't be able to gauge the distance to something in front of you until you're right up on it. So you know that something is 15 minutes away, but you can't actually sense that distance/time span ahead of you, so 15 minutes away doesn't feel much different than 30 minutes."*

One obvious solution to this problem is for us to measure how long things actually take us, so that we can reset our internal time clocks, but for Timebenders, this isn't as easy as it sounds. If we set out to measure a simple activity like getting ready in the morning, we can fall at the first hurdle – we pick up our smartphone to start the timer, and find ourselves reading our emails or checking the weather. It took me weeks of failed attempts. When I eventually managed to measure myself getting showered, dressed and ready at normal speed, I was quite shocked to discover it takes me 28 minutes. I would have guessed around 15 minutes. It looks like I underestimated by almost 50% (though if I'd been in a hurry, I'd have been ready a lot quicker).

Timekeepers don't see time as elastic. If they get asked to take on an extra task, they first have to drop another one off their list. The expression "*If you want something done, ask a busy person*" actually means "Find a Timebender," because we are happy to slip in an extra task, and enjoy the challenge of getting everything done.

It's tempting to be a little envious of Timekeepers, imagining that they have calm and measured lives, allowing plenty of time for everything, and going to bed at the same time every night with a sense of serene satisfaction and a neatly ticked-off list. But you'd be wrong. Because life doesn't always fit in with a Timekeeper's arrangements – it sometimes throws in a banana skin just for fun. When their well-laid plans skid out of control they feel seriously out of sorts, because it just isn't in their nature to speed up. All too often their vision of a perfect day is spoiled. Timebenders, on the other hand, can easily slow down or accelerate, and so we have more of a chance of going to bed at the same time every night – even though it is always later than we planned.

But before we let ourselves off the hook, maybe it's time to face up to an uncomfortable truth?

Our Secret Scale of Acceptable Lateness

"I have noticed that the people who are late are often so much jollier than the people who have to wait for them."
E.V. LUCAS – ENGLISH HUMORIST

Will I be late for my own funeral? I'm tempted to get the last laugh and copy actress Elizabeth Taylor, famous for her lack of punctuality, who left instructions that her coffin should appear 15 minutes after her funeral service was due to start. Being late for my own wedding, on the other hand, is one of the few times when it **is** acceptable – we all know that the

bride doesn't arrive on time. But I wouldn't dream of being late for my grandmother's funeral, or my daughter's wedding – which shows that I can "Just Do It" when I really want to.

Let's face it, we Timebenders have a secret we don't want our partners to know – we don't even admit it to ourselves. Hidden deep down in our minds, we check everything out on our "Secret Scale of Acceptable Lateness." Or putting it another way, we CAN be on time when it matters. We all know how to do it when we believe it really counts. Some things are so important we wouldn't dream of being late. We build in a big margin of error to make sure we arrive on time. Shock horror – we might even arrive early! The international flight. The important job interview. The court appearance. We all know there are some things we would never risk being late for. But what do we put at the other end of the scale?

We all have a list inside our heads which might read something like this:

- o Always be early for:
  - Airline check-in
  - Weddings and funerals
  - Job interviews
  - Court appearances

- o Really should be on time for:
  - Work / College
  - Taking kids to school
  - Doctor's appointment
  - Client meeting

- o Would like to be on time for:
  - Exercise class
  - Choir
  - Hairdresser
  - Physio

- Don't really need to be on time for:
    Meeting friends
    Family parties
    BBQs

- Could always be late for:
    Dinner parties
    Music gigs
    Movies

This is why we don't think of ourselves as always late. We can all be early when we have to, and these are the moments we like to remember. We all bury deep in our memories the "*Oh sh*t!*" moments when we wanted to sink through the floor with embarrassment. Which is why sometimes people we know as lifelong Timebenders can be so totally in denial: "*Me! Always late? You're kidding! I can be on time if it really matters.*"

It's easy to remember when we were just in time, and very easy to forget when we were just a few minutes late. If a class doesn't start until I get there, I imagine I am in time, and don't think anything of it. It takes a shock before I realize the truth. It was only when my teacher announced, "*Here's Grace, so we can start now,*" that I realized, to my embarrassment, that they always waited for me. It made me move the class up my Secret Scale of Acceptable Lateness, and start arriving just in time, instead of a bit late.

The big problem is that the people whom we love the most are the ones who we don't mind being late for. We can relax – we know they won't hold it against us. But we might not realize that it's always the same people we keep waiting – our friends and family. So although we see ourselves as being only late occasionally, they see us as ALWAYS late.

They might not say anything to our faces, but they will always add on a time lag to any appointment we make. My wonderful step-mum has stopped asking me when I am going to

MY TOP! SECRET · SCALE · OF · ACCEPTABLE LATENESS

ALWAYS BE EARLY FOR:

Airline check-in
Weddings & funerals
Job interviews
Court appearances

Really should be on TIME for:

Work / College
Taking kids to school
Doctor's appointment
Client meeting

Would like to be on time for:

Exercise class
Choir
Hairdresser
Physio

don't really need to be on time for:

Meeting friends
Family parties
BBQs

COULD **ALWAYS** BE LATE FOR:

Dinner parties
Music gigs
Movies

arrive, she just says *"Call me when you're on your way."* My equally lovely mother-in-law, who was a very clever cook, would make meals which kept warm in the oven for hours without spoiling, so when we arrived flustered, with tall stories of hold-ups on the journey, she welcomed us with open arms and told us that our timing was perfect and the casserole was just ready. It wasn't until after she passed away that my father-in-law let the cat out of the bag – they would always add an hour onto any arrival time we ever gave them.

It seems crazy to treat the people I love in this way – these are the people I really want to spend more time with – so why do I behave like this? After all, from the day I learned how to read a clock, I was taught the importance of being on time.

The Blame Game

"My commitment to being early isn't just good for me.
It's good for the nation. It's good for the world."
                                                BARACK OBAMA

In the Western World, clocks and schedules rule our lives,
and we learn that being early is good, and being late is bad.
From the first day we arrived late at school we were taught that
punctuality is important. If we rush in late, the people who arrived early can get very irritated, though we often don't realize
this. Most are too civil to say anything, but they might ex-
change glances with each other, or look accusingly in our direction. They tend to take it personally, as Brent Beshore explains
in Forbes Magazine, *"Being on the receiving end of tardiness used to
be a major source of frustration. It made me feel unimportant, dis-
missed, and disrespected."*

Although the people who have to wait for us are usually far too
polite to tell us how they feel, they will use the anonymity of the
internet to let off steam about our lateness, and the motives they
attribute to us. There are some incredibly angry people out
there, who find our behavior inexcusable, and feel bitter about
our lack of consideration for their feelings. ScribblePouit writes:
*"Chronically late persons are selfish and have no excuses whatsoever.
You can explain why you are late, saying how terrible you feel, but in
the end you value your own time more than the time of the person waiting for you."*

Zenith writes: *"I wouldn't dream of keeping another person waiting for me because that is so intensely disrespectful. Late people are so self-absorbed with their own wants, needs and desires that anyone else becomes a total afterthought, even if we end up sitting alone in a restaurant or bar or meeting room waiting for them."*

Ted explains: *"People who are a few minutes late are sending a pretty clear passive-aggressive message of disrespect. They are sending a big F-U to everybody else in the room."*

Not everyone hides their identity. Katie Sarott writes in "Chicago Now": *"I wholeheartedly believe that people who are chronically late are extremely selfish. Excuses about not having enough time mean you didn't properly budget your day to fit me into your already existing schedule. You shouldn't have made the plans in the first place!"*

The people who wait for us can often assume we are late because we like the feeling of power, or because we just don't care about keeping them waiting. They don't want to hear our feeble explanation that we never set out with the intention of being late. It just happened as a result of the unconscious choices we made along the way. Timebender ML explains what our problem is: *"You're not thinking about negatively impacting people… because you're not going to be late. Until you realize you are, but it's too late, and then you feel horrible."*

The sad truth is that we rarely experience what it feels like to have to wait for someone, so it's easy to ignore the fact that we are being totally inconsiderate. We tend to be in denial because we can be punctual for events near the top of our Secret Scale of Acceptable Lateness. We also assume that if we only just miss our deadlines, that makes it OK, as HeartBlossoms spells out: *"It's one thing to be five minutes late once in a while, but it's quite another to be late all the time, sometimes by as much as an hour. That's just rude."* We make an important distinction between minutes and hours. Jenni is sometimes late herself, but considers her (ex)friend's lateness inexcusable:

> *"One of my best friends throughout my childhood and into my mid-twenties was constantly hours late for everything. Sometimes I would be at her house, and she would call a friend and say that we were ten minutes away – then jump in the shower! At that point you know it's really going to be more like an hour or two. This form of lateness is inexcusable, especially when it is constant. I, on the other hand, am often five to ten minutes late for non-work-related events – often because I underestimate the amount of traffic or the overestimate the frequency of the transit system in my city. I'll usually feel awful and text the person or persons that I'm meeting to let them know and then try to find a faster way to get there, usually by taxi (not cheap)."*

Someone who is habitually hours late may be suffering from an underlying psychological disorder such as depression or ADHD, and would be advised to seek professional advice (see Can Therapy Help?). However, before you breathe a sigh of relief if you think you don't fall into this category, you should know that ALL Timebenders can be outrageously late when two key factors come into play together – the need for real deadlines and the Secret Scale of Acceptable Lateness. If we make casual arrangements to meet up with friends and family without a specific deadline, we can end up being late by hours rather than minutes, with little thought for the people at the waiting end. Sadly, it is the people we love the most who see us at our worst.

Surprisingly little research has been done to help us understand or resolve our problem, in spite of the apparent damage to the nation. There are some staggering estimates of "the cost of lateness" quoted frequently in the Western press, designed to grab headlines and castigate our lack of punctuality. However, not only are the figures based on flimsy data, and very out of date, but the estimates are totally inconsistent. In 2012 it was claimed that the UK economy loses £9 billion a year through lateness (Fly Research); yet a 2002 survey put the US figure at $3 billion (which would have risen to only $3.83 billion by 2012 when adjusted for inflation). The numbers make no sense, yet these "facts" are still regularly quoted by journalists and bloggers.

And even if the figures were accurate, would they be valid? Calculating our average minutes of lateness assumes we are idle during that period of time – yet for a Timebender, the last minutes before a deadline are usually the busiest moments of our day. We could turn this on its head and point out that Timekeepers are usually unproductive for an average of 10 minutes before every appointment, which adds up to an even higher figure. I'm tempted to conduct a survey of the cost to the economy of people who always arrive *early*, but I doubt it would get much press coverage.

Yet is the belief in the importance of punctuality a universally-held value? Robert V. Levine, Professor of Psychology at California State University, compared the pace of life in large cities around the globe, and was able to prove that people in cities in Western Europe and Japan were the most obsessed with timeliness. His research showed that their inhabitants walked and worked faster than the rest of the world, but he also discovered that they had the highest rates of coronary heart disease – demonstrating that a fast pace of life is not necessarily better.

In Japan, any lateness on a child's school record can affect their chances of getting a place at university, so the importance of being on time is drummed into them. This can lead to tragedy – one poor schoolchild was so desperate not to be late for school that she was crushed to death in the automatic gates. Levinc's Pace of Life study showed that the slowest countries were in the Middle East and Latin America, with Mexico right at the bottom of the list. These countries see punctuality from a different perspective – they like time to relax and have fun, go with the flow and enjoy the good things in life.

Lily is a Timebender who has decided the perfect solution to her struggle with lateness is to emigrate: *"I want to move to Ikaria, Greece. Not just because people live extra-long, extra healthy lives there, but because nobody cares about being on time, so it literally is NOT POSSIBLE to be late."*

Yet does punctuality always achieve the best outcome? How often do you meet a creative person who is always early? When do writers ever meet their deadlines? David Godwin, literary agent for a list of bestselling writers including Ben Okri and Arundhati Roy, says, *"Nearly all authors are late. Probably 10 per-cent are on time, but most are late for all kinds of perfectly obvious reasons."*

Jennifer Saunders, who wrote the ground-breaking comedy series "Absolutely Fabulous," used to bring half-completed scripts to rehearsals and finish them on set just before filming. It didn't do much for the actors' nerves, but she produced some brilliant and original work.

Helen Fielding, creator of the global bestseller "Bridget Jones' Diary," says she can never finish a manuscript until it is *"So late for the deadline that it is snatched from my hands by someone very annoyed-looking."* And this is nothing new – Charles Dodgson worried about time, just like his White Rabbit in Alice in Wonderland. *"I am getting into habits of unpunctuality and must try to make a fresh start,"* he wrote in 1856. In Alice's magical world he could simply manipulate the clock – if only we could do the same.

Clocking Up the Minutes

"The clock has decided to take time into its own hands."
ANON

I dream of one day owning a vintage Rolex, because old mechanical watches can unexpectedly gain time, and I might occasionally surprise myself by arriving early. I sometimes try to achieve the same result, when I fly back from another time zone, by changing the time on my watch without looking too closely. I hope I might set it slightly fast, but I'm taking a bit of a gamble, because I might make it slow, which would be a disaster. The accuracy of quartz watches has robbed us of a great excuse for being late, though this apology could backfire – when US President George Washington's secretary arrived late for a meeting, and blamed his watch for his tardiness, Washington famously replied, *"Then you must get another watch, or I another secretary."*

If only there was a way we could trick our minds into being early. Danni found a strategy that works for her:

> *"I deliberately put appointments into the calendar on my phone 15 minutes to a half hour earlier than they really are. Because of the time denial in my head, I generally forget I've done this (even though I do it almost all the time), and so even if I leave 'late' for the appointment in my calendar, I'm still on time."*

61

Like many Timebenders, I used to keep my watch and car clock 10 minutes fast, hoping to trigger half my brain into thinking, *"OMG, is that the time!!"* Unfortunately, the other half of my brain always knew better, so I couldn't fool myself. I then became terrified of putting my watch right again – in case I might still imagine it was 10 minutes fast. I just ended up doing subtraction sums in my head all the time. I also stressed out several of my Timekeeper friends, who would panic if they caught a glimpse of my watch or car clock, because they thought we were running ten minutes late. Occasionally my partner would helpfully put my car clock right, for which he was unjustly abused. My relationship with time became very complicated. In the end, I went to a therapist, who told me "Time is your friend, not your enemy," and persuaded me to set my watch, and other clocks, to the proper time. I'll share my experiences of therapy with you later in the book.

Thanks to the Demon Deadline Shaver, once we check the time before leaving for an everyday appointment, we can't help trimming off a few minutes, and so inevitably arrive a few minutes late. Tamsin explains that there can be a cost to this behavior:

> *"I seem to view any deadline as a challenge which I have to beat. If I'm shopping and I've had to pay for my parking in advance, I never manage to get back to the car until the very last minute I've paid for, and sometime get a penalty ticket because I've pushed myself over the deadline."*

If our appointment is with a Timebender, we have an unspoken understanding that we will both be a bit late, which is great. But if we are meeting up with a Timekeeper it's a different story, as journalist Rachel Matthews explains:

> *"If I'm seeing a friend, I'll leave 10 minutes earlier than needed and be at the station half an hour before my train de-*

> *parts, with my tickets already picked up. If I have to get up early for a flight then my alarm will go off an hour earlier, just in case I don't get up straight away."*

Timekeepers get very frustrated with us, because they can't understand why we don't stick to the time we agreed. We can't explain to them that we'll be late for WHATEVER TIME WE HAVE ARRANGED. One strategy is to tell people that we can't be sure what time we will arrive, but that it will be "*Somewhere between 1pm and 1:15pm.*" Sadly, this usually means we end up arriving by the latest time suggested (or probably a few minutes after). Our Demon Deadline Shaver always seems to push us right to the very end of the time limit.

Timekeepers who have spotted this have come to the logical conclusion that they should lie to us about the start time, especially for events low down on our Secret Scale of Acceptable Lateness, for which we might be an hour late. It seems like a great idea, but sadly, over time it makes things even worse. Our deadlines need to be real, and once we find we have been lied to, we will assume this happens all the time, so our Demon Deadline Shaver will start to factor this in. Fifi found this to her cost:

> *"My husband is always late, so I've started compensating by lying to him about when things start. I give him a time that's 30 minutes early. The problem is, he's cottoned on, and the panic monster no longer shows up for him unless I'm freaking out. So now, I not only have to give the wrong time, I have to fake panic when we aren't actually late yet."*

When I commuted to work by rail, my Demon Deadline Shaver kept me fit by making me run for my train every day. My dream scenario would be to drive, park, buy a ticket and stroll onto the platform just as the train arrived. Needless to say, I very rarely achieved this, which made mornings very stressful.

It seemed that the only way to catch a train in good time was to miss the one before. Come to think of it, trains are to blame for the whole problem...

The only way to catch a train is to miss the one before!

A Brief History of Time

"Better three hours too soon than a minute too late."
WILLIAM SHAKESPEARE

Until the development of the railroads in the 19th century, nobody could be sure what "the right time" was. When people measured time by the shadow on a sundial, no-one could say whether you were five minutes early or five minutes late. Timebenders were still safe when the first clocks appeared, because they were invented by monks who needed to know the times of matins and vespers, so they simply rang a bell to mark the hours. In fact, the word clock comes from "clocca," the Latin word for bell. (If you want to see an amazing example, the clock on Salisbury Cathedral in England was made in 1386 and is still working – it has no clock face, just a bell that chimes every hour.) The minute hand was invented to meet the needs of astronomers, but back in the 16th century no clocks were accurate, so you still couldn't be accused of being late. It also helped that no-one could agree what the time was, since it was calculated against the sun at noon, which moved as you travelled from East to West.

It wasn't until the invention of the pendulum clock in 1657 that clocks improved their accuracy, but it was the opening of the first passenger railway from Liverpool to Manchester in 1830 that fundamentally changed the importance of punctuality in our lives. Once the new railway networks began to link up across England, accurate timekeeping suddenly became a matter of life and death, because trains ran according to the local time at the town where their journey originated. For example, the southbound train on the Birmingham & Gloucester Railway ran on Birmingham time, which was 59 seconds ahead of the northbound train, which took its time from Cheltenham.

By 1840 engineers became seriously concerned about potential accidents and proposed that all railways should adopt London time. The idea of a single unified time zone made good sense in a small country like Britain, where the time difference between westerly Plymouth and easterly London was only 16 minutes. By November 1840 the Great Western Railway had adopted London time, and the other railway companies quickly followed.

While "Railway Time" made a huge improvement to the safety of rail travel, it didn't stop people missing their trains because, although stationmasters and train guards were issued with tables which enabled them to convert local time to London time, town clocks were notoriously inexact. Accurate time became so valuable that people who lived near Greenwich Meridian were able to make their living by it. John Belville, an astronomer at the Royal Greenwich Observatory, used to visit a network of London subscribers each week between 1836 and 1856 to sell them a glimpse of his pocket watch.

Outside London, rail passengers continued to be confused about the correct time until 1852, when technology took a hand in things. The amazing new electromagnetic clock at Greenwich was linked by telegraph to the Electric Time Company in the City of London, which then transmitted the time signal around the entire railway network. Predictably, this started up a conflict between London and the regions, and before it was resolved there was a crazy period in the mid-1800s when many towns had two different clock times, local time and "railway time." Surprisingly, even telegraph time was not quite as reliable as you might imagine, due to problems maintaining the wires, which is why John Belville's wife, and then his daughter, continued to make a living touting round his original pocket watch. It wasn't until TIM, the Speaking Clock, began to provide the correct time via the telephone in 1936, "*at the third stroke, precisely,*" that Belville's daughter Ruth finally retired, aged 86.

In countries that cross multiple time zones, the problem persisted. Fourteen passengers died when two trains collided at speed near Pawtucket, Rhode Island, USA in August 1853 because the conductors were working to different clock times. The accident impressed itself on the public consciousness because it was the first train crash ever to be photographed, and the shocking image was featured in the New York Illustrated News. In spite of public concern, there was no easy solution, because the huge span of the USA was divided into hundreds of different railway times. It took until 1883 before four standard time zones for the continental United States were introduced in Chicago, from where the telegraph lines transmitted time signals to all major cities.

The geographic area of Russia is 75% larger than the USA, creating an even greater challenge, and it wasn't until 1919, after the Revolution, that the country was finally divided into time zones. Today Russia is divided into a record 11 time zones across its vast landmass, and their boundaries are still being redrawn right up to the present day.

Since our lives are dominated by the need to be on time, it seems hard to believe that the modern concept of punctuality only began in 1852 in England. It wasn't until 1884 that the idea went global when Scottish engineer, Sir Sandford Fleming, successfully proposed that the world should be divided into 24 Standard Time Zones. From then on, everything speeded up, as the Timekeepers gained control of the industrialized world. Within only a century, by 1955, the atomic clock took over from the sun, and by 1960 the US and the UK got together to create Co-ordinated Universal Time, which means that punctual people can now have the satisfaction of telling you how late you are to the nearest Leap Second.

But there is another man who played a major part in the Western world's obsession with timekeeping – Fred W. Taylor. As a foreman at the MidVale Steel Company in the USA, in 1880 he observed how inefficient workers were if left to their own devices. With the aid of a stopwatch he started analyzing each element of their work, and using the "Principles of Scientific Management" he demonstrated to industrialists how they could increase their profits by improving efficiency.

His work turned up the speed dial on the huge US manufacturing machine, and set the standards which still drive Western economy. Every millisecond now has a value, and "time is money" has become the mantra of the modern world. Fred Taylor's biographer, Robert Kanigel, sees him as the man who *"helped instill in us the fierce, unholy obsession with time, order, productivity and efficiency that marks our age. Foreign visitors to America often remark on the rushed, breathless quality of our lives."* He is perhaps the reason why the image of a frantic Harold Lloyd, hanging desperately from the hands of a skyscraper clock in the film "Safety Last!" (1923), is one of the great icons of the twentieth century.

Yet even today, the concept of time in industrialized countries isn't quite as accurate as you might expect. When Prof. Levine measured people's walking speed for his global "Pace of Life" experiment, he had his researchers in each country check the accuracy of 15 clocks, in randomly selected downtown banks, against the correct time as reported by the telephone company. No prizes for guessing which country came top of the list for accuracy – Switzerland runs like clockwork – the UK was in 13th place, the USA 20th and Canada 22nd out of a total of 31 countries.

But the clock is not the only invention which has made life difficult for Timebenders.

The Timebender's Big Black Hole

"I wasted time, and now doth time waste me."
WILLIAM SHAKESPEARE

Tim Berners-Lee has a lot to answer for. His invention has evolved into a monster which eats time on a scale never before known to man. If we Timebenders let down our guard for an instant, it swallows us up and drowns us. It can make hours seem like minutes as it tempts us ever further into its clutches, laying little trails of gingerbread into the forest, which we follow until we have no idea where we are. The world wide web is a Timebender's worst nightmare.

Until 1990, a Timebender's life must have been very simple – though we didn't realize it at the time. We could lose ourselves in a book, or get carried away listening to music, or watching tv, but we were still moving around in a physical universe. We had to turn the page, change the record, find the remote to switch channels – all moments when we could return to reality for an instant, and have the chance to glance at the clock on the wall, and remember where we were, and what we should have been doing instead. We never drifted out too far, and could still swim for the shore before we were lost at sea.

The internet has changed all that. Now we can get drawn in by the gingerbread cookie trail with just a slight movement of a finger. Whatever we are doing, the distractions just keep popping up. That enticing little sound that tells us a new message has arrived; the pop up that tells us a friend is online and free to chat; the adverts that hover around our vision, tempting us to find out which celebrity lied about what – how can we resist?

Even if we are determined to ignore all distractions, the Google gorgon can still entrap us. We can be (for once) focused on the task in hand, when we decide to just check a date, or how to spell a name – and we are lost. I blame Amazon too – when they first tempted us with the words "*People who viewed this item, also viewed...*" they took the first steps in learning how to create the magic spells that Timebenders are powerless to resist.

But where there's a need, there's a business opportunity, and help is available. Fred Stutzman, an academic from Carnegie Mellon University, USA, created the first in a wide range of productivity apps to help us avoid online procrastination. Their internet blocker Freedom locks you out of your apps and websites for a set time. Freedom users report gaining an average of 2.5 hours of productive time each day. (Ironically, Google and Microsoft are among its biggest clients.) Fred says it isn't our fault – we are social beings, so we can't just expect our willpower to change a hundred thousand years of human evolution. So instead of looking for Free Wi-Fi in cafes, we should start looking for Wi-Fi Free instead.

A creative agency based in Barcelona, Herraizsoto, has gone a step further, and now sells the tool they came up with to help their own difficulties with getting writers to concentrate. Not only does their productivity tool – OMMWriter – get rid of all distractions on your screen, it gives you swirly patterns and pastel colors to type on instead of a white page, and even offers you an optional typewriter sound, which they've found can encourage you to keep typing. Your choice of music is very limited – they know from experience that even choosing a playlist can take your eye off the ball. The tool then gives no other options – not even Autocorrect. You can check your spelling once you have downloaded your text into your normal word processing software. They describe it as "*A distraction-free writing environment, where you can close the door behind you, to focus on your writing in peace.*"

Since Timebenders make up one fifth of the global market, it's not surprising that over a million copies of OMMWriter have been sold, and there are loads more free alternatives such as FocusWriter and WriteMonkey. At last we have gone full circle – we have a technological development which allows us to cancel out the effects of technology. Now that's progress!

But now I think I've an apology to make.

Excuses, Excuses!

"I'm sorry I'm late, but I didn't really want to come."
ANON

A pologizing for being late is one of the big moral dilemmas, if you're a Timebender. It's a bit like farting, or eating the last brownie – do you mention it, or do you just keep quiet and hope no-one has noticed? Do you come clean and apologize, or is it OK to blame it on the dog? Marilyn Monroe was one of the few people who didn't feel the need to lie: *"I am invariably late for appointments – sometimes as much as two hours. I've tried to change my ways, but the things that make me late are too strong, and too pleasing."*

Telling the truth seems a bit uncaring and makes us feel a bit stupid, which is why we never actually admit. *"Sorry I'm late, but I just didn't leave home on time."* It seems much less embarrassing to give a good excuse, but just how far can you go? If we drove for a few moments behind a driver under instruction, or slowed briefly behind a school bus, or followed a funeral cortege for a short distance, we consider

it lucky, because we can weave quite a convincing excuse around a grain of truth. In fact, we can be so convincing, that we can even persuade ourselves that it's true.

On the other hand, it can be frustrating if we DO get held up by such inconvenient obstructions, because we have to think of another excuse that will explain our double dose of lateness. Traffic jams and road works are a more believable excuse if we are more than 10 minutes late, but it's best to make sure no-one else uses the same route.

Cell phones are a great invention for Timebenders, because sending a message five minutes before you are due to arrive, to say you've been held up, is a great way of getting any embarrassment out of the way. It gives us two advantages. Firstly, if you are going to bend the truth, you can do it without having to look into people's eyes. And secondly, when you turn up 10 or even 20 minutes later, you actually feel like you are on time, which is brilliant. But do try to avoid giving a specific time of arrival, or you might underestimate, and end up late all over again.

If you are ALWAYS late for something you do regularly – like getting to work, or the 8am biology class, or driving the kids to school – it's best to say nothing. There isn't really any excuse you can give that will convince anybody, so it's best just to keep quiet and not give any reason at all. They aren't going to believe you, whatever excuse you come up with.

I once worked with someone who arrived 15 minutes late for work every day of the week and always had an excuse. He commuted from the London suburbs and always blamed his lateness on train delays, but his excuses became so outlandish that in the office his (secret) nickname was "Badgers on the track." It gave me an insight into what it is like to be on the receiving end of a Timebender's excuses – and it wasn't much fun. As we shared an office, I used to brace myself for the morning routine. I could set my watch by him. He would rush in through the door 15 minutes late, fix me with a beady eye, and deliver some long and elaborate story to explain why he'd been delayed. I realized that he would judge his success by whether he thought I looked convinced or not. This became rather tedious. Once, over a drink, I plucked up the courage to ask him the obvious question – if his trains always made him 15 minutes late, why didn't he leave the house 15 minutes earlier and catch the previous train? He smiled with relief, and I thought he was finally going to admit, *"My name is David and I am a lateoholic."* Instead he told me that actually his son was always very slow getting out of bed, and as he had to take him to school, it always made him late. (A true Timebender in denial – it wasn't his fault at all!)

So think twice before coming up with excuses if you are usually late. The people you are trying to convince with your tall stories, or your little white lies, might just be sniggering behind your back.

If you DO give an excuse, this list might come in handy:

Ten Top Excuses for Being Late for Work

1. Stuck in traffic
2. Overslept / alarm didn't go off
3. Lost car keys / wallet / phone
4. Car trouble
    o Flat battery
    o Flat tire
    o Something leaking
    o Ran out of fuel
5. Train was delayed
6. Bus didn't turn up

7. Someone was ill / visit to the doctor
8. Pet problem
9. Power cut
10. Stopped by police

A word of warning, if you are the sort of person who likes to share – think twice before telling others about your constant battle with the clock. Once they know your secret, they will be watching out for signs of weakness. They might never have spotted that you always magically appear at the door just as the meeting or class is about to start, but once you admit it, they will notice every time. Worse still, they will point it out to others. They will find it amusing and start making comments. Your cover will be blown. You will become the focus of attention. Even the manager or teacher will make comments about the time you arrive. And everyone will see you as "always late," even if sometimes you are on time.

So let's stop making excuses and look at some strategies to avoid being late.

PART TWO

The Timebender's Toolbox

Tried and Tested Tips to Get You There on Time

It's a relief to know that we're not alone – 20% of the population has a problem with timekeeping. We aren't late on purpose, but we feel uncomfortable about finishing things, and we can't aim to be early. We approach important jobs the wrong way around, we are usually over-confident about the speed we can get things done, we almost believe our own excuses, and we have a little demon in our heads who always pushes us up against a deadline – and sometimes past it.

So what can we do to improve our lives and the lives of the people around us, if waving a stern finger at ourselves has little effect? We all have a few strategies up our sleeve which we can use when we really need them. In this next section, I'd like to share my toolbox of tips with you. I've divided them into what I consider to be our two Timebending Superpowers.

Deadlines

> *"Depend upon it, sir, when a man knows he is to be hanged in a fortnight, it concentrates his mind wonderfully."*
>
> SAMUEL JOHNSON

Timebenders respond to deadlines like dogs when you get their leash out – we jump up off the sofa and leap into action. We have an extraordinary subconscious response which knows when a deadline is getting serious. It is like a temperature gauge inside our heads, which starts off cool and blue, and slowly starts to turn red as the deadline gets closer. Once it is almost at boiling point and in danger of exploding, we move through the invisible wall into that other world where our Timebender's superpower kicks in – we become amazing. We find we can concentrate 100% on the task, and plough through the work in an astonishing way.

Because of the rush to the finishing line, when we hit the deadline, we are often left with the feeling that, if only we'd had a little more time, we could have done a better job. We remember all the time we wasted at the beginning and wish we could add it back at the end. We can't imagine why we didn't get down to work a bit sooner. We swear that next time we will start earlier. We promise ourselves that we will learn from this experience, and in future will allow enough time to do the job even better. But next time we just can't stop ourselves from slogging through the same crazy old Timebending routine.

So how can we turn this behavior to our advantage? How can we trigger this superpower of ours? Here are some tricks to keep up your Timebending sleeve.

Deadline Tip 1: Always Ask for a Deadline

"When do you need this by?" Six little words that make all the difference. Do not assume that other people grasp how crucial deadlines are to us. Remember that Timekeepers actively dislike deadlines. They like to feel calm and in control, and tight deadlines make them very stressed and uncomfortable. They will (un)helpfully tell you there is no deadline, if a job isn't urgent. Unfortunately, if people tell you it doesn't matter when you get a job done, then you're probably never going to get around to doing it. Yet at some point it WILL matter that you haven't done it, and then they might get annoyed, and say they can't believe you haven't done it yet. So always try to get the deadline out on the table right at the start. If there is no deadline, then suggest one yourself. Even though you came up with it, it becomes a public commitment, which makes it real and external.

Deadline Tip 2: Involve Other People

Since our deadlines need to be real and external, it can help if we involve other people. If others are tied into the same deadline, you don't have to rely on your own internal thermometer.

Having a partner who can get stressed when a deadline is getting dangerously close is a great help. When they get cross and start shouting, you will know that it's definitely time to get moving. Unfortunately, while this works for you, it's not much fun for them.

A good ruse we've already looked at is to offer to give someone a lift, because then your deadline is the time you have arranged to meet them, not the event itself. You will, of course, be a few minutes late picking them up, but hopefully you'll have built in a bit of extra time to allow for this. This works particularly well for regular commitments, because these are the ones our Demon Deadline Shaver slowly cuts down to the bone.

Spending money to solve the problem can pay off, especially as it can save you money in the end. Paying a bookkeeper to help you with your accounts is a good example. Tax offices such as the UK's Inland Revenue and the US's IRS understand how to motivate Timebenders – they keep turning the screw to keep up the pressure. In the USA, if you file your accounts more than 60 days after the due date, the penalty can be up to 100% of your unpaid tax. In the UK, they first charge you £100 for a missed deadline, but as this isn't enough to motivate the real procrastinators, they keep upping the charge until finally you pay the whole amount twice. These Revenue Offices are actually doing us a big favor – the first deadline is usually enough to motivate us to get the job done and out of the way.

Other deadline buddies can be much more fun. If you want to get more exercise, but can never get yourself to the gym, then try hiring a personal trainer, as you won't want to waste your money by turning up late. I hate tidying the house, but also hate living in a mess, so my solution is to invite people over. I can clear up in no time when I am expecting guests, but no matter how many good resolutions I make, I can't bring myself to do it on a routine basis. Unfortunately, this means that if I don't find people to invite every week, I end up living in a sort of nest, surrounded by things I am just about to put away but haven't quite gotten around to. This doesn't bother me too much, but it has caused a few problems – the pile of papers on the microwave almost caught fire once, and if people called unexpectedly, I was very reluctant to invite them in. Eventually I found a better solution – I hired a cleaner for an hour a week. She's great value, because every week I zip around the house before she arrives, tidying up and putting everything away. (Cleaners clean – only *you* can tidy your own stuff.)

Deadline Tip 3: Take off your Watch

Be warned – this idea takes quite a bit of courage. Since we know we always squeeze our deadlines, this trick confuses our brains by getting rid of clocks and watches, so that our Demon Deadline Shaver can't calculate how much time can be trimmed.

You start by measuring your regular daily activities, which is tricky for a Timebender. Once you've managed to measure how long it takes you to get ready in the morning, you're ready to try this.

Here is an example of how it works. Let's say you know you need to leave the house at 8:30am, and it takes you 30 minutes to get ready (not forgetting transition time). Put an alarm on your phone for 8am. Once your alarm sounds, don't look at

your phone again until you have left home and shut the door firmly behind you. Not knowing the exact time will make you nervous, and you will find you subconsciously allow a few moments extra, just in case. If you try this trick, you might find you have done something unheard of – you might have left home a few minutes earlier than necessary.

If you want to try an experiment, instead of looking at the time once you're on your way, check the time just BEFORE you shut the door. If you still have a minute or two in hand, you will be amazed at the things your Demon Deadline Shaver will suddenly tell you that you absolutely MUST do before you leave. You can find yourself totally convinced you need to grab a snack; or check you've remembered your phone; or go to the bathroom.

Another chance to use this tip is when catching trains. If your service runs fairly frequently, then don't look up the train schedule – just arrive at the station and catch the next train. If you don't have a deadline, then your Demon can't get to work, and you might even arrive at the station early. Some Timebenders find the best cure for lateness is never to wear a watch. It sounds scary, but it might work for you.

Deadline Tip 4: Make a Ulysses Contract

Ulysses was a Greek superhero, but he had a weakness – and you won't be surprised to hear that it was women. He couldn't resist the song of the Sirens – enticing creatures who could lure

85

a man to his doom. He knew he'd never get home to his wife Penelope if he heard their voices, and he had to sail right past their island. Being a Superhero, he had a super idea – he had himself tied to the mast, so that he couldn't be tempted by the Sirens' song. He knew he wouldn't have power to resist temptation, so he tied his hands in advance.

How can we learn from this Superhero? The Ulysses Contract works best on really super-sized tasks, like writing a book or a thesis. It also needs you to be courageous and determined to reach your goal.

1. First decide which milestones you will need to meet if you are to achieve your goal. Then place a bet with a friend that you will achieve these, and if you fail, you agree to pay an amount of money to a charity which THEY can nominate – ideally for a cause which you don't support. (If you still have a checkbook, give them the post-dated check up front.) Get them to swear to stick to the terms, no matter how hard you might argue later that you've changed your mind. (If you can't find a friend who will do this, then ask an enemy instead.)

2. Here is an alternative option that doesn't involve gambling. You'll need to find someone who is interested in your project – they don't need to be a close friend. Give them a schedule of your target dates, and clearly lay out each goal. Ask them to be your "deadline buddy," who will check what you have achieved at each milestone; and review what you will be doing by the next. Put the dates in both your diaries – it only needs a phone call. By tying your pal in, you are making the deadlines external and real.

3. Tie yourself to the mast metaphorically by creating a distraction-free space for yourself. If you have the means, build yourself a writing shed. If you aren't one of the super-rich, find somewhere in your home, or a friend's home, or a public place like a coffee shop or library, where you are able to concentrate. (Do avoid the kitchen, as it's too full of temptations.)

4. Go naked. Victor Hugo used to give his clothes to his valet and write in the nude, so that he couldn't go out to the bar with his friends. You may find this idea a bit too cold for your climate, but it could give you some ideas. Don't we all feel naked without our smartphones these days?

5. Download a productivity app, to stop you going online or using your smartphone for as long as you want to concentrate.

The most audacious Ulysses contract ever drawn up was between a pair of brilliant comedians – the "Absolutely Fabulous" Dawn French and Jennifer Saunders. Jennifer had been notoriously last minute with her scripts for their tv series, so it was no great surprise that she was late with the filmscript for "Ab Fab – The Movie." She started it in 2006, and still hadn't finished it in 2014, eight years later. Dawn French was getting desperate, as she knew Jennifer was brilliant, but an extreme Timebender. *"I knew that she was never going to finish it, though she really wanted to. We agreed a one-way bet. She could give me £100,000 or the Ab Fab script by the end of 2014."* The bet was very public, as it was made on live radio, but a year is a long time, and the contract didn't seem to be working. *"It was getting later and later in the year and I said to her, 'Jen, I am honestly going to take your money.' I even spoke to her husband and told him to get the checkbook out,"* she said.

They met again in mid-December and Dawn asked Jen if she had the finished script. *"She had a bit of fear in her eyes but she said, 'Yes I have' and she slapped it down on the table. I looked through and there was Patsy and Edina all there. I shook her hand, but when I got out of the room and looked further, I realized the first 30 pages had scenes but the rest of the pages just said, 'Blah, blah, blah blah, blah.'"* She realized she had been tricked, and confronted Jennifer, who swore she would have the screenplay finished by the end of the year. *"I was away in Mexico on New Year's Eve and 11:55pm there was a ping on my husband's email, and there it was. It was delivered just five minutes before midnight!"* This Ulysses contract really paid off, as it resulted in the biggest British film of the year, which took £30M at the box office.

Deadline Tip 5: Commit to Doing a Draft Before the Finished Article

Sometimes we don't want to start a large or important piece of work because we are worried that it won't be perfect. If you have an elephant-sized task, then tell the intended recipient that you will first let them have a draft (not forgetting to mention when you will let them have it). Drafts come easily to Time-benders, because while we are spending 80% of the time not getting on with the job, we are quietly mulling over things, and we usually have a pretty good idea of the rough shape of what we want to create. Once you have scribbled down your initial ideas, you'll have a reasonable outline for the finished piece, and as a bonus, once you've submitted your draft, you should get feedback on whether the idea is OK or not. And if it's not OK – well, it was only meant to be a draft.

Once you have done a rough draft, you are halfway to the finishing line. You can fill in the details surprisingly quickly when you've done all the thinking up front, and you lose your

fear of failure once you know what sort of reception the finished article will get. This is a great way of avoiding the procrastinator's Catch 22 of putting off a task because you're daunted by wanting it to be perfect, but then realizing that, the longer you've delayed it, the greater people's expectations will be.

Deadline Tip 6: Break a Task into Mini-Deadlines

We do 80% of our work in the last 20% of time left before a deadline, so the more deadlines we have, the better. Instead of trying to eat an elephant in one sitting, we need to make elephant sandwiches. It's a lot easier to calculate the time it takes to complete small sections, so there's less chance of making an elephant-sized mistake. If we miscalculate the deadline on an enormous project, we could find our estimate is out by weeks, and even though we have superpowers, not even Timebenders can wind back the clock.

Mini-deadlines can give you more time for fun, as well as making you more productive. As we know, our deadlines must be real, so you could arrange to meet with a friend, or book a session at the gym, or make any other commitment in the external world. Although you are taking time out, you'll find your focus increases as the mini-deadline approaches. You'll be amazed at the ideas you can have in those final five minutes when you should be getting ready to leave. As soon as you know you must stop, you'll wish you could carry on. As well as being more productive, we are often at our most creative when we're up against the wire, so the more deadlines we face, the more chance we have of coming up with brilliant ideas.

Deadline Tip 7: Set Your Deadlines When You're Calm

We know we are not good at measuring time, but unfortunately this problem gets worse once the adrenaline starts pumping. The closer the deadline, the more we shave the time allocation, so plan your schedule well ahead of the event. When we are calm, we make sensible decisions and build in buffer zones. When we are stressed and under time-pressure, we can become wildly unrealistic. When we go into panic mode, much of the blood in our brains moves into our limbs ready for flight or fight, and we can no longer think straight.

The day before going on vacation, you can easily foresee it will take you at least two hours to pack your bag, half an hour to get dressed, and an hour to make sure the house is tidy and secure, and you know you should check in two hours early. This is the sensible moment to set your alarm and book your taxi/Uber. If you wait until the morning, when you are already starting to feel anxious, you will believe you can race around and do everything in twenty minutes. Since you know deep down that you are going to squeeze the time anyway, make sure you have left something to squeeze.

Deadline Tip 8: Create a False Ending

Lizards have a clever trick if they are caught by a predator – they can detach their tail, and leave it wriggling enticingly as they scuttle off under the nearest rock. (Impressively, they can later grow a new one.) In a similar way, it's really helpful to have something that isn't actually going to kill you if you drop it when you are under pressure. The Timebenders' equivalent to a lizard's tail is having something non-vital to do before the deadline, which can be dropped off and abandoned if necessary.

This distracts the part of our brain which feels uncomfortable with closure. We can outsmart our subconscious by adding something to the end of the list of tasks which actually isn't vital. Making a coffee, watering the houseplants – you'll know what works for you. But it's important to make the final task something pleasant, to keep up your momentum. If you leave your least favorite job until last, like cleaning your shoes, you might unconsciously slow down before you reach it.

Sadly, my "lizard's tail" is usually breakfast. Each morning, when I get up, I look forward to my favorite breakfast – muesli, yoghurt, berries and nuts – I love it! Every morning I tell myself I will be ready and dressed ten minutes before I must leave the house, so that I can sit down and enjoy a good bowlful. And almost every morning I always seem to be surprised to find that I have no choice but to rush out the door ten minutes late, grabbing a cereal bar. I realize that I could change the order in which I get ready, and eat my breakfast first – but I have scary visions of rushing out the house in my pajamas. I do sometimes manage to eat my bowlful on the run while I am getting dressed, but this still requires me to find the time to go to the kitchen and prepare it. Mostly I only get to enjoy my favorite breakfast on my days off – usually around lunchtime.

Your lizard's tail can be added during the journey – you could plan to post a letter or stop to buy a paper on the way. Another false ending which has worked for me is factoring in the time to stop for fuel, when I have just enough to get me to my destination. Fortunately, there is always a bit left in the tank when my car tells me I am running on empty, but I wish I hadn't found this out, because now it is a bit like playing Russian Roulette.

Any woman knows that make-up can be left until later. When commuting to work by train, I was fascinated to see women shamelessly going through their full make-up routine. I'm not so bold. I have been known to put on my lipstick in traffic jams – but I'm pleased to say I've never done it while driving in the fast lane of the expressway. Nor have I attempted to imitate the unfortunate Megan Mariah Barnes, who was famously arrested after rear-ending a pick-up truck in Key West, Florida, while attempting to shave her bikini area!

Deadline Tip 9: Set Up an Earlier Deadline Before a Big Event

When the consequences of being late can be unthinkable, try to get your real and external deadline as early in the chain of events as possible. This helps to limit both the level and length of your stress. For example, if you are catching a flight, avoid driving to the airport if you possibly can, because you don't want your first real deadline to be the time the check-in desk closes. If you're five minutes late (as usual), you've lost the whole vacation. It would be far less stressful to create an earlier deadline by ordering a taxi/Uber, or arranging for a friend to drive you. Keeping a friend or taxi waiting for five minutes while you run back inside for your flip flops won't be the end of the world, because you will have built in a buffer zone. If you have no choice but to drive yourself to an important event, then see if you can create an earlier deadline. If you are going to a wedding, or a funeral, or a big-ticket concert, could you arrange to meet family or friends for a meal or drink beforehand? Could you drop your car at someone's house and share the last part of the journey with them? If you have no option but to drive yourself, consider booking yourself into a hotel the night before – the cost could well be worth it.

Deadline Tip 10: Have Something to Do While You're Waiting

We know we have a real problem with being early, because we see it as a waste of time, so make sure you always have something to do while you are waiting. Smartphones make this easy – if you don't have messages to read, you can always scroll through photos, catch up with the news, update your social media or learn a language. If you want to try to kick the adrenaline habit and live life at a slower pace, then use the time to practice meditation and mindfulness. If you are a people person, then arrange to meet someone before the event begins.

The trick is to focus on the activity, and promise yourself a certain amount of time to do it. Tell yourself, "*I need to get to my class by 8:45am so that I can catch up with Becky.*" That way you can get your adrenaline high by being late for your "pre-event activity" rather than the event itself. Don't tell yourself, "*I'll try to get to the class 15 minutes EARLY, to catch up with Becky.*" If you focus on the idea of being early, your Demon Deadline Shaver will resist this and make you late.

Summary

▶ Deadline Tip 1: Always ask for a Deadline

▶ Deadline Tip 2: Involve Other People

▶ Deadline Tip 3: Take off your Watch

▶ Deadline Tip 4: Make a Ulysses Contract

▶ Deadline Tip 5: Commit to Doing a Draft Before the Finished Article

▶ Deadline Tip 6: Break a Task into Mini-Deadlines

▶ Deadline Tip 7: Set Your Deadlines When You're Calm

▶ Deadline Tip 8: Create a False Ending

▶ Deadline Tip 9: Set Up an Earlier Deadline Before a Big Event

▶ Deadline Tip 10: Have Something to Do While You're Waiting

Distractions

"It's impossible to enjoy idling unless one has plenty of work to do."

JEROME K. JEROME

Timebenders turn Stephen Covey on his head by doing our important and urgent tasks last, but how can we turn this contrary behavior to our advantage? Our second superpower is to make sure that when we are putting something off, there is something else useful waiting to catch our eye. How many of us find that we can't start get started on a big project without first tidying our desk or sharpening all our tools? The most tedious jobs in the world start to look attractive when we shouldn't be doing them, so make sure they are visible when we are in this moment of madness. "Out of sight, out of mind" is the opposite of what we are trying to achieve here.

And here's the good news. Once we understand that we only really knuckle down to a job when we feel the adrenaline kicking in, it also means that there's no point in starting a job early. We can enjoy distractions with a clear conscience. Instead of telling your friends you can't join them to watch the big game on TV because you really think you should be getting down to work, you can go out and enjoy yourself. You will feel it in your gut once the deadline is dangerously close, and then you'll have no problem turning down the invitation. When you start to recognize the difference between *"I really think I ought to start putting some time into this"* and *"OMG, I'm going to be LAAATE!"* then life can be a lot more fun.

If you *do* sit down at your desk in advance of a deadline, and start working on a task before you need to, you will prove to yourself the truth of the expression *"Work expands to fill the time available,"* because the chance of a true Timebender finishing a job early is zero. We will go back over our work, revise it, change our minds, and dither until the deadline clock starts ticking loudly. At this point we will really start to focus, work with full concentration, and hit that deadline like a champion skier ending a downhill run.

Distraction Tip 1: Always Have an Untidy Desk

Litter your desk with all the unfinished tasks and boring jobs you can't be bothered to do. Scatter them around so that as many as possible are within your vision. Then, when you sit down to start some serious work on a big project, your Fairy Godmother will wave her magic wand and all that boring stuff will be transformed into the most fascinating tasks in the world. One after another they will catch your eye, and you will decide to "just fill in my expense sheet" or "send this invoice," or even "complete my tax return." If you don't have any unfinished

paperwork to complete, you will look around the room and spot that the printer nccds a new cartridge, or that your screen needs cleaning.

Distraction Tip 2: Start with the Fun Stuff and Do the Work Later

If you are thinking about going for a run, meeting a friend for lunch, or popping out to the shops, just do it. You won't get your work done any quicker just because you allocate more time to it – you will just put it off for longer. Once the deadline clock is ticking loudly in your ears, you'll be too scared to think about having fun, so the temptation won't arise. If you decide to be virtuous and sit down at your desk before you really have to, you will only dither. You might get other jobs done, but you won't actually produce anything worthwhile on your main task, because you'll end up reworking it.

There are two important guidelines to follow. Firstly, always make a small start on the task, so that your brain can start to mull over the problem. Secondly, find distractions which are mildly amusing rather than fully absorbing. Running, walking, and gardening all meet the criteria, and computer games and Sudoku are particularly effective, because they free up your subconscious mind to work on the problem, while you are enjoying yourself.

Distraction Tip 3: Give Yourself a Double Bind

The Double Bind is an old trick which can be usefully applied to Timebending. It means that if you only have one choice, you can choose to do it – or not. But if you have a choice between two options, you tend to pick one of them. Successful author Geoff Dyer explains how it works for him: "*If I've only got an idea for one book, I tend to do nothing. If an idea for an-*

other book then comes along, I'm torn between both, but the knowledge that I'm 'bunking off' from one of the two serves as a kind of motor for getting going on the other one." The fact that Geoff has written 15 books shows that this is a good trick. (One of his books is called "Out of Sheer Rage," which is about his not being able to get down to writing a book about D.H. Lawrence, who was himself a procrastinator.) So if you have been putting off decorating the bathroom, start thinking about decorating the spare bedroom as well, and see if this helps you to get the paint brushes out. You'll come to welcome the big tasks which you aren't looking forward to doing, like completing an assignment, or filling in your quarterly tax return. You know you'll get them done by the deadline, but you'll get a lot of other smaller jobs out of the way first.

Once you become expert at using the double-bind, you might find yourself signing up for other activities which have deadlines, just for the sake of it. You might start a course of study, or join a book club and commit to reading a book each month. Another way to apply this idea would be to volunteer for one-off tasks which you don't enjoy – like writing up the minutes of a meeting, or washing the dog, or searching for something in the attic. Avoiding doing something that you dislike is a great way of motivating yourself to do the tasks you have been putting off.

Distraction Tip 4: Look for the Carrots

Never try to force yourself to do something by mentally waving a big stick – you'll only look for distractions. Instead, try to find a carrot to hang on the end of it – look for ways to make the task seem more attractive. Give

GIVE YOURSELF A TREAT TO AIM FOR

yourself something to aim for.

If you want to get more exercise, volunteer to walk the neighbor's dog. If you've been putting off decorating the bathroom, invite your favorite aunt to come and stay in a month's time. If you keep putting off going to the gym, get a guest pass and invite a friend. If you hate cleaning the house, invite some friends round and you'll whiz through the work in no time. If you don't want to write that thesis, promise yourself a treat for every section you get done. You know best which reward will motivate you – and if you're a healthy eater, it might even be a carrot!

Distraction Tip 5: Start Early

The day is full of distractions waiting to tempt us away from our task. As soon as our eyes fall on any alternative to what we should be doing, it becomes very tempting. Our best chance to

get started is when the world is at its quietest – first thing in the morning. If your task is desk-based, and you work from home, the best strategy is to go straight there. Don't shower, or you'll suddenly decide to descale the taps. Don't get dressed, or you'll start tidying your bedroom. Don't even have breakfast. Just start. Set yourself a target – *"No breakfast until I have done xyz work."* If you find you are still working in your pajamas by lunchtime, you should see it as a sign of success.

If you aren't a morning person, then you might find the opposite works for you – work into the night when it's quiet and the rest of the world has gone to bed. This is more of a challenge, because the day will have already thrown many distractions in your path, and it is harder to clear them out of the way. But on the plus side, darkness can be calming, and bed is a great target.

Distraction Tip 6: Don't Interrupt the Flow

If by some miracle we are concentrating and "in the flow," we should try to avoid stopping at all costs. Yes – even for the bathroom. Because stopping not only breaks our concentration; it also opens the door to all those interruptions clamoring to get in. If we simply go and make a cup of coffee, we can find we have started on a trail of distraction traps – talking to office colleagues, emptying the dishwasher, checking our emails – which can keep us chasing around until lunchtime.

> *"When I start to write a new novel, sorting and tidying all my drawers suddenly becomes amazingly attractive."*
> KATE ATKINSON – AUTHOR

We all have a natural concentration span, and taking a break refreshes our brains, so of course we have to stop sometimes. The point is to avoid interruptions when we are in mid-flow. If our work involves sitting at a computer, we know the various health risks, so frequent breaks are important, but it's worth being aware of the avoidable distraction traps.

We all know how enticing our computers and phones can be, so hopefully we have turned off all the alerts and reminders. But have we gone as far as installing a productivity app, which means that, if we need to look something up, we have to make a note for later? If you're really desperate, "Write or Die" is an app which will punish you by starting to delete what you have written, if you don't meet the target you have set yourself. You can choose your level of punishment from **Gentle** to **Kamikaze**, but once you stop writing, the screen starts to change color and then your words disappear one by one.

Offices are full of unavoidable distractions, but there are a few steps we can take. Can we persuade someone to bring us a coffee, to save us being drawn into the gossip around the drinks machine? Can we wear noise-cancelling earphones if we are working in a busy environment? Even if it's quiet, wearing a full set of headphones is a great signal to other people that we are concentrating and don't want to be disturbed – we don't even need to plug them in. Another option is to wear one of those baseball caps displaying the words "DO NOT DISTURB" – originally introduced by companies with open plan offices, but now more often worn when snoozing on the beach.

There is another way I sometimes apply this tip. If I have been to a meeting and am driving back to the office, I need to go straight to my desk and write up my notes, but I'm easily distracted. This can be a bit disastrous, as I might not get down to it for a day or so, and by then I've forgotten most of the important stuff. So I now make it a habit to find somewhere on the route, where I can stop and write everything down, before my thoughts get interrupted. I've even sat outside and written my notes in the car, which must look rather odd to the neighbors.

Distraction Tip 7: Get Ready the Night Before

In the morning, if we must leave home by a certain time, it's too easy to get side-tracked by deciding what to wear, or what to put in your bag. So, since we often look for an excuse to delay going to bed, it can be helpful to get things ready the evening before. If you are a man who starts work early, shaving before you go to bed can save you ten minutes in the morning. If you're on the school run, you might be able to get the clothes and lunches ready before you fall into bed. If you're going to a meeting, don't wait to sort out your paperwork until the last minute, because you are likely to be in a panic and won't be able to think straight. Get your papers ready the night before, so you can just grab your bag and go. If you're going on a long journey, programming your GPS and refueling the car the day before is a helpful way to save yourself extra stress.

Distraction Tip 8: Beware the Voodoo Power of Lists

Be careful what you write on your lists, as they have strange powers. They're useful as memory joggers, but beware of writing a list of the MAJOR tasks you're unlikely to forget, such as rewiring the house or publishing your memoirs. Once you've noted these job down, you're unlikely ever to do them – unless there is a deadline. The bigger the project, the more it will become an elephant you will simply ignore, rather than an elephant sandwich you can tackle in a few minutes. If you want to get a project done, then just write down the first action you need to take to get it started, like "Buy paint" or "Bring box of memorabilia down from the attic." Then you can leave the stuff lying around, so that it will catch your eye when you should be doing something else.

The most ineffective list of all is the one that is written for us by someone else. The more official-looking the list, the more we start to see it as a waving finger telling us what to do, and the more we will want to ignore it and do something else entirely. Steve gives a perfect example of this: *"When I first got married my wife brought home a whiteboard on which we could list the jobs that needed to be done. About a year later it disappeared. Just before our silver wedding anniversary I found the whiteboard in our garage. There were about 20 jobs on it. None of them had been done – and most of them still needed to be done."* The problem with lists is that they move a job from something you can pick up as a distraction, to a MUST DO. Unless there's a deadline, we avoid MUST DO tasks at all costs.

Distraction Tip 9: Calm Your Inner Rebel

Eliminating all distractions in order to get down to the task we have been avoiding can leave that rebellious teenager inside our heads looking for something to do. So keep them quiet by playing them soothing music.

Research has shown that baroque music, played at its normal time signature, slows your heart rate and pulse in time with the beat. Amazingly, playing the music backwards still has the same effect. When you are in this relaxed but alert state, your mind is able to concentrate more easily.

Catherine Lux, when writing her dissertation in 16 hours, was surprised by the music which helped to sustain her through the night. *"I listened to Glenn Miller's Little Brown Jug for a few hours on repeat. It was the only song I could listen to that made me concentrate. I have no clue why."*

On-line music streaming services such as Spotify or iTunes have "Concentration" or "Focus" playlists which include white noise and nature sounds as well as modern and classical options. You can choose the type of music that might work for you, though it's usually best to avoid vocals, as the words can break though into your conscious brain. Gregorian chants work for some people, because the words are in Latin. The younger you are, the louder you will want the volume, but you need to set it at the right level for concentration, rather than distraction. Keeping the sound just below your conscious awareness is usually the best option.

Distraction Tip 10: Beware Bad Habits

Distractions come in many shapes and sizes. If you have a bad habit that is easy to indulge while you are working, like smoking, vaping, drinking coffee, or snacking, then you have an extra challenge. Lighting up a cigarette, sipping a drink, or reaching for the cookie jar can be an almost automatic action.

Before I start work I'll just take a look in the fridge

The sad thing is that, if you are concentrating, you don't really notice the pleasure.

Looking in the fridge or cupboard for something to nibble is a lot more tempting than cleaning the cupboard under the sink when we are working near the kitchen. My weakness is nuts, and if I make the mistake of working with a bag of nuts within reach, I crunch through the whole lot, one after another, without even tasting them. What a waste of calories. Since I don't notice what I'm eating, I'd be better off munching through some sticks of celery – but somehow, I never do. I'm not a gum chewer, but I can see the benefits. If your mouth is busy chewing gum, it can somehow leave the rest of your head free to concentrate.

Summary

▶ Distraction Tip 1: Always Have an Untidy Desk

▶ Distraction Tip 2: Start with the Fun Stuff and Do the Work Later

▶ Distraction Tip 3: Give Yourself a Double Bind

▶ Distraction Tip 4: Look for the Carrots

▶ Distraction Tip 5: Start Early

▶ Distraction Tip 6: Don't Interrupt the Flow

▶ Distraction Tip 7: Get Ready the Night Before

▶ Distraction Tip 8: Beware the Voodoo Power of Lists

▶ Distraction Tip 9: Calm Your Inner Rebel

▶ Distraction Tip 10: Beware Bad Habits

PART THREE

Timebending Through Life

How Do We Change Over Time?

I can't remember when I first became aware of my tendency to be late – perhaps because it was my poor parents' responsibility to make sure I was on time? I do remember that the penalty for being late for assembly at elementary school was to keep my hat and coat on until the morning break, because it happened to me more than once. Clearly it didn't cure me!

Once we start to grow up, and become responsible for ourselves, the battle begins. Getting to classes on time, studying for exams, commuting to work or working from home, enjoying our family life, going on vacation – all offer new challenges.

Once we choose a partner, we start to become aware of the differences between our attitude to time and theirs, and this can often be a trigger for trouble. The solution isn't living alone, however, because this can prove to be the greatest test of all.

This next section looks at the specific issues we have to deal with at home and at work, and delves into the toolbox of Timebending tips, to see which ones might be helpful.

Family Life

A s Timebenders we have enough trouble managing our own schedules, so being responsible for our children's timekeeping multiplies the problem alarmingly. From that very first baby's cry, Timebending parents discover that they have lost all control over time. In the beginning, time is so short and there is so much to do that even Timekeepers find themselves apologizing for being late: As Leena explains: *"Even when I plan to leave early, it doesn't happen. Nothing ever goes as it's supposed to. It's not something we do on purpose. We want to be there on time – it's just that life with little ones is totally unpredictable."*

But Timebenders still find the time to post on social media, however busy we are. Sharing photos of toddlers on Instagram is a great way of putting off dealing with household chores. Twitter is a great forum for sharing the chaos, as this apology for being late reveals: *"Baby had a poop explosion. I went to change her and got poop on her head. Then she needed a bath. My toddler insisted he also had poop on his head, and he needed a bath too."* But not all the difficulties of arriving on time are disastrous, and maybe punctuality isn't always the top priority when children are very young. *"We decided to walk to your house. It should have taken three minutes, but on the walk, we saw an ant, a dandelion, cars driving by, rocks, gardens, a neighbor waving, our mailbox, a crack in the sidewalk, a tree, and grass. Now we're 30 minutes late."*

As children grow, life becomes packed with more and more deadlines, and being late is pretty much unavoidable once par-

ents return to work. The daily school run can be a daily torment for Timebender parents. Are you one of the parents who screeches up the road ten minutes late every day, breaking speed limits and causing the locals to ask for a speed trap? Will your children be one of the last to be collected? Will you always be parked ten minutes' walk down the road from the school, because you only just made it on time? How can you avoid shaving this daily deadline, once you know exactly how much time it takes? Jade, a Timebending mother of two, loves her children and doesn't want them to be waiting for her after school every day, so she always saves her emails and phone calls until she is waiting at the school gates, and deals with them while sitting in her car. Her children know she'll always be there on time, though sometimes they have to wait for her to finish before she drives them home.

Schools can be very unsympathetic towards this problem, and sometimes come up with draconian solutions. Parents at the Holy Trinity Primary School in Gravesend, UK, were shocked to receive a letter from their school to say that they would be fined £1 for every five minutes they are late picking up their children. Furthermore, if a child was uncollected 30 minutes after school finishes, Social Services would be informed. Head Teacher Denise Gibbs-Naguar sees the problem from the child's point of view: *"School finishes at 3:30pm but it is becoming an increasingly regular experience to have a significant num-*

THE SCHOOL RUN

ber of children still on site at 4pm. Pupils who are collected late often exhibit signs of anxiety and distress as they don't know where their parent/carer is, and are worried that something may have happened to them."

Once your children are old enough to travel to school on their own, you still have to get them up and ready to leave home each morning. No-one has yet invented the Ejector-Bed for getting teenagers up, but Deidre, who was a teacher herself and had no time to waste in the morning, found that a wet towel on the feet under the duvet worked pretty well. It also had lasting effect – she told me she only had to apply the penalty once – after that she could get the same result by just mentioning towels.

Mira is a very fond mother, and all her daughter Maya would need to plead from under the duvet was "*five more minutes…*" and her mum wouldn't have the heart to get her up, so she would be late for school. However, when Maya joined the prestigious San Francisco Girls' Choir, timekeeping became vital. There was keen competition to get into the choir, and if you arrived late three times in a term, you lost your place. Mira was never late delivering Maya to choir rehearsals – the Timebenders' Secret Scale of Acceptable Lateness means we can be on time when we choose.

Persuading children to study for exams can create huge tensions. It's very hard for parents to recognize that Timebending children will never concentrate until the deadline is looming. Rick still regrets the summer boating trip he missed as a schoolboy, after he failed his exams. His parents insisted that he needed to start revising again immediately, so he reluctantly gave up his place on the boat to another friend. He then wasted the whole week, torturing himself by imagining the fun they were having without him – the extra study time made no difference whatsoever to his exam results.

Jason has two daughters – one is a Timebender like himself, and the other is a Timekeeper, like his wife Jo. When it comes to exam revision, Jo knows what to do. First, she sits down with her Timebending daughter and schedules her revision with her, since she knows her daughter will be completely unrealistic about how long everything will take. Then she creates a real and external deadline, such as – *"If you don't get this revision done, you can't go out with your best friend on the last day of the vacation."* Jason is very relieved that it isn't left up to him, as he can only empathize.

Families demonstrate the truth of Jung's theory that our attitude to time is due to nature, rather than nurture. Wendy has three children, James is the oldest, and a Timekeeper like his parents, but Kate and Mark are Timebenders, who needed lots of shouting to get them up and on their way to school. Once her son James passed his test and was old enough to drive his siblings to school, Wendy was surprised to find that he would simply drive off without them if they weren't ready. This had a very noticeable impact on their timekeeping. Ironically, Kate is now a teacher, and would never dream of being late for her class. Her son Tom, on the other hand, finds it really hard to get up in the morning... Round and round we go.

Top Tips for Family Life

▶ Have Something to Do While You're Waiting (Deadline Tip 10)

▶ Look for the Carrots (Distraction Tip 4)

▶ Get Ready the Night Before (Distraction Tip 7)

▶ Calm Your Inner Rebel (Distraction Tip 9)

Relationships

"Few things tend to alienate friendship more than a want of punctuality."

WILLIAM HAZLITT, ENGLISH WRITER

In the early stages of a new relationship, those rose-tinted specs prevent us from noticing the imperfections in our loved ones, and lateness can just seem like a charming quirk. When we find someone who gives us unconditional love, we imagine that we can be our true selves, and Timebenders hope that any lack of punctuality will be understood and forgiven. But once the honeymoon period is over, the frustrations can build up until the dam bursts and accusation starts to fly, *"...and another thing – you're ALWAYS late!!"*

Although we know we aren't late on purpose, our waiting partners find it hard to believe that we always THINK we're going to be on time. When we appear remorseful, but never actually change our behavior, they can understandably assume that we don't care about their feelings. Our Secret Scale of Acceptable Lateness reinforces this, because our loved ones can start to notice that we can be on time for work or other appointments, but we are always late for them. Once the cracks appear in a relationship, lack of punctuality can take on huge significance, and can be the cause of break ups. The only solution is mutual understanding.

"Lateness can indeed hurt those we love, and we should try and prevent it as much as possible. However, being hurt is determined not merely by the lover who is unpunctual, but also by the way the punctual partner interprets the lover's lateness."

AARON BEN-ZEEV, PH.D., AUTHOR OF "THE ARC OF LOVE: HOW OUR ROMANTIC LIVES CHANGE OVER TIME."

An Extreme Timekeeper married to an Extreme Timebender is a nightmare scenario. If this is you, then you will be only too aware that timekeeping can be a trigger for conflict in your relationship. The stress levels experienced by the Timekeeper are likely to cause them to make an early exit – either through the door, or in a box. Sadly, Angela learned the hard way: *"I lost the absolute best relationship of my life, the one that I could honestly see lasting 'till the end of time, because I let my life drag in absolutely every activity and never attempted to change, despite constant self-loathing. I took things for granted. And I realize it's like you feel you can't quit smoking until doctor tells you that you have a terminal disease – and then you stop almost painlessly and realize it wasn't so difficult after all. But it is too late by that time."* If your partner is still with you, then this should be a great incentive to change your behavior.

When someone is constantly "working late at the office," the partner who is waiting at home can start to question the validity of the excuse. Anna's husband Hussain worked in finance, and on Fridays he rarely left the office before 8pm, because he had to complete weekly reports. Once she had fed their two young children and put them to bed, Anna would sit waiting for her husband to come home, feeling anxious and unhappy, and wondering if she could really trust him. Telling him how she felt didn't have any effect on his behavior. It wasn't until she understood the psychology of lateness that she found the solution – she created a real external deadline by telling him what time she would be serving the dinner and sticking to it. The mental picture of eating a lonely reheated dinner gave Hussain an incentive to finish his work, and usually did the trick.

OMG!! YOU'RE HERE!!!

Andrea and Jamie found out early in their relationship that, in spite of all they had in common, they had very different attitudes to time. She was a great cook, he had a good wine cellar, and they both loved entertaining, but she would still be busy in the kitchen ten minutes before the guests were due to arrive, and he would get pretty hot under the collar. She finally had to explain to him, *"Look, I will always be ready IN time, but not BEFORE time, so just relax with a glass of wine and stop worrying."*

But when exactly were their guests expected to arrive? Cultural norms vary between countries, so check this out if you don't want to cause offence. In the US or UK, it is normal to arrive 10-15 minutes late for a dinner invitation, but a German host will be offended if you don't arrive on the dot. And, although the French frequently arrive 10 minutes late for business meetings, the chef might throw a tantrum if you arrive late for dinner. The further South you go, the more relaxed the attitude to time – in Latin countries you should never turn up early, but an hour late isn't seen as rude.

I rely on my guests being 10 minutes late, as my house usually looks like a bomb has exploded half an hour before guests are due to arrive. Getting dressed and tidying the house used to be the last jobs on my list, but my partner has gently encouraged me over the years to put these essential jobs earlier in the schedule, so that I don't greet my guests in scruffy clothes and a messy house, with a look of horror on my face and the words, *"Oh my God!! You're HERE!!!"*

It really helps if your friends are Timebenders too, because you will have an unspoken understanding that no-one will arrive on time. On the other hand, if they are the sort of people that judge you harshly if you're late, you aren't likely to remain friends for long. Jean and Ray went on a trip with a couple who turned out to be Extreme Timekeepers, and who were excessively early for any start time they had agreed. If they'd arranged to meet for breakfast in the hotel at 8am, their friends would already be sitting outside in the car by 7:45am, looking disapproving. Their punctuality anxiety spoiled the whole vacation, and ultimately their friendship.

As we have seen, Timebenders rarely admit to the real reason for their lateness, and can come up with very convincing excuses but, over time, these can wear rather thin. When a friend has been kept standing in the rain, or missed the start of a concert, more than once, they can start to question not just the excuses, but also the honesty of the person trotting them out. Christine used to enjoy interesting discussions with Brenda, a woman she met at her annual librarian's conference, and they started meeting up occasionally for lunch. She believed Brenda's excuse for being half an hour late the first time they met, but when the same thing happened three times in a row, Christine decided to turn down any more invitations. She said, *"I felt really upset that she didn't think about the impact her behavior had on me, and I also lost any trust in the reasons she gave for why she was late."*

So if you want to maintain a friendship with a Timekeeper, try to be as honest as you can about why you are late, and if the truth is embarrassing, then maybe it will help to bring the relationship higher up your Secret Scale of Acceptable Lateness. The Guidelines for Partners section at the end of this book may give you both some useful suggestions.

Top Tip for Relationships

Get your partner or friends to read this book – at least they can learn that you aren't driving them mad on purpose.

Timebending at College

E scaping from home into student life brings freedom from the structure, timekeeping and discipline of family and school, but at the same time, it brings some of the largest and longest external deadlines we will ever face – end of year exams, dissertations, theses and finals.

Timebenders can get into terrible difficulties when deadlines are measured in years rather than hours, as Jonathan knows: *"I just submitted an incomplete Ph.D. thesis. I submitted an introduction, three good chapters, a fourth very bad draft chapter and no conclusion. I just did not have the time. I did not sleep during the last 48 hours before submission. However, I know I can do it, if they give me some more time and another chance."*

This is why all universities have strict penalties for late submissions, ranging from a 40% cap on marks, to a straight zero. They do their best to make the deadlines as real and non-negotiable as possible. Perhaps this is because the authorities know that once we get to college, there are more distractions to tempt us away from studying than ever before. Sports, music, drinking, eating, and good conversation are on offer everywhere, and it takes a lot of self-discipline for Timebenders to focus on a goal which is far away in the future. As Tim Urban so brilliantly illustrates in his 2016 TED Talk, our Instant Gratification Monkey finds it very easy to take over from our Rational Decision Maker. Students are typically advised to write priority lists, create schedules, and devise wall charts, but Time-

benders will only do these things as a distraction to starting work, and once done, probably won't look at them again.

Richard remembers how much time he wasted as a student: *"I really shouldn't have picked Chemical Engineering as my degree subject, as I found it really boring, and spent most of my three years at university avoiding it. However, I got amazingly good at playing my guitar, and spent hours and hours practicing. Once I graduated, I didn't pick up the guitar again for years."*

Some students spend so much time being distracted that they ought to be awarded a degree in the subject. Distraction activities can come in all shapes and sizes – including "weighing the cat," as we heard earlier. It's amazing the ideas which seem logical at the time. One anonymous Timebender explains: *"Whilst writing my dissertation at Bournemouth University, I entered the race to become President of our Students' Union. I had no intention of ever winning and no interest in the job at all. I went on to campaign for a whole week just before my deadline. Overall, I spent approximately four days writing my dissertation. Co-incidentally I have to submit one of my essays before I can graduate. This is due in tomorrow and I am nowhere near done."*

121

Motivating students to be punctual is an art in itself, and some solutions are surprisingly effective – especially when they are devised by the students themselves. Maya is in a competitive Poetry Slam Team, made up of eight students who need to develop a very close working relationship. They come from a variety of backgrounds, and don't all have the same attitude to punctuality – especially the guys. Maya explained to me how they have solved the problem: *"If someone arrives late, we all lose valuable rehearsal time, so we have agreed a penalty – one press-up for every minute of lateness. However, the whole team has to get down and do them. You avoid being late because you care about the team. The worst penalty we've all suffered is 36 press-ups, but things have improved, and now it's usually less than 10."*

Top Tips for Student Life

▶ Always Ask for a Deadline (Deadline Tip 1)

▶ Break a Task into Mini-Deadlines (Deadline Tip 6)

▶ Make a Ulysses Contract (Deadline Tip 4)

▶ Always Have an Untidy Desk (Distraction Tip 1)

▶ Start with the Fun Stuff and Do the Work Later (Distraction Tip 2)

▶ Don't Interrupt the Flow (Distraction Tip 6)

▶ Beware the Voodoo Power of Lists (Distraction Tip 8)

▶ Calm Your Inner Rebel (Distraction Tip 9)

▶ Beware of Bad Habits (Distraction Tip 10)

Travel

Timebenders love vacations – no deadlines and no stress – but preparations for travel can be our greatest nightmare. We need to get EVERYTHING finished, which is very stressful to anyone with an aversion to closure. First, we must tie up all the loose ends in our work and home life, and then decide what to pack, even though we're not sure what the weather will be like or what we will be doing. We therefore dither about what to put in our cases until the very last minute, which makes us really anxious if we need to catch a flight, knowing that if we're ten minutes late for the check-in, the whole vacation will be ruined. (I can feel my heart beating faster just writing this.)

One answer is to stay at home – an option chosen by many Timebenders, who never quite get around to booking a vacation. For those who manage to get away, there are a few tips that can make vacations less stressful. Firstly, try to create an early deadline. You know you are going to panic, and will overrun the time limit – just don't do it at the airport, when there is no leeway left. Call a taxi in plenty of time, and panic before it arrives. That's when to make the final decisions of what to take – should you find space for your sun hat or winter coat- just in case. What does your case weigh? Have you got your passport, currency/extra cash, tickets, phone, stopped the mail, turned off the water and lowered the heating? If you don't have an external deadline, your Demon Deadline Shaver starts paring away the buffer zones you have built in, and you don't actually put your suitcases in the car until an hour after you told yourself you would, so the whole journey is stressful, and you begin your vacation a nervous wreck.

Airlines ask you to allow plenty of time for delays, though I can't help thinking that being told to check-in three hours before a transatlantic flight seems designed to get you to spend more money at the airport. However, not trusting the advised check-in time is dangerous, because the next deadline is the closure of the check-in desk. If it's within your budget, booking a hotel at the airport the night before means that, even if you don't get there until midnight, at least you'll be on time for your flight the next morning.

Jane, whose Timebending husband Murphy fitted the cat door just before her son's christening, has had some hugely stressful starts to her family vacation. She remembers her terror the time he sped down the shoulder of the highway past a huge traffic jam, with the children in the car, when they were in dan-

ger of missing the plane. She could never persuade him to leave home early enough to allow for delays, but she has found a solution that works brilliantly. She buys family membership passes to the Airport VIP Lounge, where they get free food and drink, a good view of the runway, and free access to on-line games and entertainment. Her husband now sets off willingly, three hours early, and everyone is happy.

Top Tips for Travel

▶ Involve Other People (Deadline Tip 2)

▶ Take Off Your Watch (Deadline Tip 3)

▶ Set Your Deadlines When You're Calm (Deadline Tip 7)

▶ Create a False Ending (Deadline Tip 8)

▶ Set Up an Earlier Deadline Before a Big Event (Deadline Tip 9)

▶ Have Something to Do While You're Waiting (Deadline Tip 10)

▶ Look for the Carrots (Distraction Tip 4)

▶ Get Ready the Night Before (Distraction Tip 7)

Hobbies and Pastimes

Timebenders love pastimes, especially when we should be doing something else! They are a welcome relief in our adrenaline-filled days, and have the added bonus of feeling like a forbidden pleasure. However, it is very easy for us to get distracted and never get around to the hobbies we would like to pursue.

Sadly, Timebenders always need a deadline – even for things we do for fun. Our tendency to avoid finishing things means that our lives can be littered with unfinished books; the paraphernalia of incomplete projects; abandoned exercise equipment; and a lot of good intentions which have never been realized.

The good news is that there are many ways to resolve this. Since we make up 20% of the population, there are plenty of other people like us, and the way to solve the problem is by pulling together. If you want to finish more books, then join a book club, so that you will make time for reading – and hopefully get to the last page just in time for the meeting. If you love art or crafts, but never manage to prioritize the time for creativity, then look for kindred spirits and arrange to meet regularly so that you can work together. You don't need a teacher – it's just a way to ensure you put aside a block of time. Whatever your interest, you are likely to find an existing group to join – just search meetup.com or other sites to find what's happening in your area. If you draw a blank, then it is easy to set up your

127

own Meetup Group, and a local bar or coffee shop should be happy to let you reserve a table on a regular basis for group activities such as knitting; writing poetry; learning a language or playing Scrabble.

The days of lockdown showed us we could all meet up through the internet, though we also discovered how easy it was to fritter away our time and get distracted from our real goals. Virtual meetups are great, but the best online groups for Timebenders are those which hold time-limited events – they might run competitions; or host webinars; or have a Top Ten List which changes each month. There are innumerable writing communities which encourage aspiring authors and poets by setting topics to work on; photography clubs and art groups in which members tackle projects and then share their images; and music sites where amateur composers and songwriters vote on each other's compositions. Online courses that issue weekly assignments and give marks and feedback are also ideal for Timebenders who need external motivation. While the UK-based Open University is geared towards academic qualifications, it also offers short courses on photography, languages, creative writing, art history and other general subjects. If music is your passion, Berklee Online and the Academy of Contemporary Music can offer you relationships with a tutor and fellow students online. Thanks to coronavirus the market is booming, and you can now find online courses and group activities on any subject imaginable.

Physical activity like running or cycling is another hobby that can be sabotaged by our tendency to get distracted. *"I'll go for a walk once I have finished my ..."* is usually a guarantee that you will never do it. Hopefully, you have resisted buying an exercise bike, which by now would be collecting dust in the basement. If you've ever taken up gym membership, there is a good chance you will be one of the many Timebenders who signed up at the beginning of the year and never went again after the first three visits. If you really want to motivate yourself, you need to create some sort of a deadline. This is why six million people meet in 22 countries every Saturday morning, for a 5k Park Run, organized by local volunteers. Another way to encourage yourself is to pay for exercise classes in advance, so it costs you money if you don't turn up. Even if you just go for a fun run, there is still a chance you will put things off, as Anne B. knows: *"It took me a year to shamefully hand in sponsorship money after a fun run I took part in for a cancer charity. I just had to find some time when I could donate some goods to one of their shops and take the money in at the same time. I felt so much better when I finally paid up – especially after being so outraged when I had heard on the day of the race that a large proportion of people do not hand over their sponsorship cash."*

There is an additional problem for Timebenders who enjoy creative hobbies – they attract a load of clutter – things we decide to keep "just in case." Most Timebenders have half-completed hobbies hidden away in cupboards and basements – the models we thought we would build; wood-cutting tools; artists materials; strange musical instruments; knitting wool; sports equipment, etc. Scrapbooking means you've been storing used wrapping paper and bits of ribbon; quilt-making gives you a reason for keeping off-cuts of material; carpentry means your basement is stuffed with odd bits of wood, and jars of used screws. We're very good at starting projects, but finishing them can be a major challenge.

You might think we could just forget about our unfinished work, but you'd be surprised how much it can haunt people, as Pauline knows: *"In 1963 my dad asked me to knit him a supporters' scarf for his local team, saying that he would pay me for my work. I was 13 years old at the time, and he made the mistake of paying me in advance for my labors. You can guess that he never saw the scarf, and*

he died in 2010, aged 93, without ever seeing a return for his money.''
My friend Betty had started knitting a baby jacket before her son was born, but never completed it. It sat in a carrier bag silently reproaching her for the next thirty years. It wasn't until her daughter-in-law announced that she was pregnant that Betty fished out the bag and finally managed to finish it for her first grandchild – just before the baby had grown too large.

Not even very public deadlines can solve the problem. Nettie loved to sew, and always volunteered to make the costumes for the annual children's Christmas pantomime, which was a mammoth task. As a true Timebender, she was unrealistic about how long the work would take, and never started early enough. Each year the producer would turn pale when he realized that only half the costumes were ready by the dress rehearsal. The actors were frequently stabbed by unexpected pins, and it was never until the final matinee that the last costume was completely finished.

My hobby is gardening, but I seldom manage to enjoy the results of my work. My partner hopefully puts out two recliners

on a summer weekend and settles into one with a magazine or a book. I sct off towards the other chair, but on my way, something always seems to catch my eye, and I spend the rest of the afternoon wandering around in the sunshine, deadheading all the flowers, zapping the weeds, tying things up, cutting things down. I tell myself that when I've finished I will sit down and relax, but it never happens. I'm much happier wandering around in the sunshine with my pruning shears, because there's no danger of ever actually finishing the job. On the other hand, if I actually need to get some planting done, I get distracted and never actually make it out of the back door until it's getting dark.

Rachel lives in a flat, but finds that houseplants can be just as distracting. *"It all starts with going to fill the kettle to make our morning tea and finding there is still some left-over water in it. Rather than throw it down the sink, I wander off to find a dry houseplant, which keeps me on a trail of distraction for ages, before I suddenly remember that my partner is still upstairs, waiting hopefully for his tea."*

Top Tips for Hobbies and Pastimes

▶ Involve Other People (Deadline Tip 2)

▶ Make a Ulysses Contract (Deadline Tip 4)

▶ Have Something to Do While You're Waiting (Distraction Tip 10)

Commuting to Work

Getting to work on time is a major challenge for Time-benders, but there's good news – the more important it is to be punctual, the easier it gets. If you work in a job where you're paid for "face time" – e.g. customer services, call centers, retail, teaching, performing – then the deadline is real and immoveable.

As we know from the Secret Scale of Acceptable Lateness – when it's important, most of us can be on time. In some jobs, lateness can even be loaded with penalties – if you're paid by the hour, you can have your money docked.

A Timebender with an immoveable deadline will normally get to work on time – maybe because they have the keys to the office or shop, or because they have a classroom of students waiting for them. We might shave things a bit close, and we won't be early, but we will avoid being late, because the deadline is real.

By contrast, a job that offers flextime sounds ideal for a Timebender, but it can be a false friend. Flextime works on the principle of having "core hours" within flexible starting and finishing times. The true Timebender will be full of good intentions about getting to work early, but can rarely do it. We can't help getting distracted until we hit that immoveable deadline – the start of core hours. Timebenders on flextime are easy to spot – they rush in at the last minute, and end up leaving work later than everyone else.

If you're a "knowledge worker," being on time is less critical because, in theory, you're measured by the contribution you make, not by the hours you show up. This sounds a lot better for us, but it inevitably means we will arrive late every morning – probably by exactly the same number of minutes. This will balance out, because we will also leave work late – and probably work longer hours than we are paid for, because we just don't like to reach that moment of closure. This lets us off the hook, and our lateness will be tolerated, but outwitting our Demon Deadline Shaver will always be a battle. Giving someone a lift or meeting a colleague on the train can help. Picking up a latte on your way to work can help to get you out of the door, and also give you a lizard's tail which you can ditch if you're running late.

Getting to work on time is well worth the effort, as it is one of the most conspicuous things we do. If we are always late, our fellow workers will judge us by it and make comments – as I discovered with "Badgers on the track" David. (I wonder what they used to say about me?) Time is money in the workplace, organizations are geared towards Timekeeping, and in the Western world, lack of punctuality is seen as a very negative character trait: "*Punctuality is a sign of professionalism and helps you stand out as a reliable and trustworthy employee. Being punctual helps you establish your reputation as a dependable and consistent worker.*" Employers are unsympathetic towards our struggles with punctuality, and being sent on a Time Management course won't help, as it doesn't address our problems.

Even if we manage to leave home early, it doesn't necessarily mean we're ready to start work on time, as Mira, a university professor, explains: "*My journey into Palo Alto can vary between one and two hours, so I always leave home at 7am. I usually have more than an hour to spare before my classes start at Stanford, which is great. I make myself breakfast, and deal with some of my emails and phone calls, and print out my lesson handouts, but it doesn't mean that I am early for my students. My first lecture starts at 9:30am and it takes me five minutes to walk from my office to the class. Somehow, I never quite leave enough time, so I am always just setting up my laptop and getting out my notes when the class should be starting. If I bump into someone on my way and stop to chat, I can be embarrassingly late!*"

Getting to work is not your only struggle if you have a "people-facing" job, because if you have a regular stream of appointments, you can be fighting your Timebending tendencies all day long. The biggest challenge isn't so much starting on time, as ending each appointment on time.

Jason is a Timebending osteopath who regularly overruns by five minutes on his first appointment of the day, and never quite catches up – much to the frustration of his Timekeeping receptionists. Jason told me of a good tip he learned from a doctor friend who always over-ran his appointments. Never say "*Sorry I'm running late,*" say instead "*Thank you for waiting.*" This makes people think that you have overrun because you had a crisis to deal with.

Top Tips for Arriving at Work on Time

▶ Involve Other People (Deadline Tip 2)

▶ Take Off Your Watch (Deadline Tip 3)

▶ Create a False Ending (Deadline Tip 8)

▶ Get Ready the Night Before (Distraction Tip 7)

Working from Home

Working from home can be a huge challenge for Time-benders because having no clear boundaries, either in space or in time, is very difficult for us. Not surprisingly, there's some wonderful advice on the web about how to stop wasting time.

If you Google *"How not to get distracted working from home,"* you can browse 70 million blogs, online discussions, YouTube videos, and websites, to learn how not to waste time! Each of them says the same thing, in 70 million different ways – avoid getting distracted. For example: www.timecamp.com advises: *"Create a daily planner. Plan your day before it starts. Keep a time limit for each task. In your daily planner, mark each task with a time limit."* Ha! We Timebenders could never follow this plan.

If you want to find advice on the internet that reflects our Timebending world, then search the discussion forums and social media, because this is where most of us are spending our time. The best advice to a Timebender is *"Never attempt to work from home, unless you have real and external deadlines to keep you focused."* If you have no option, then aim to create external deadlines in whatever way you can. Pamela has a solution which only a Timebender would understand: *"When I work from home, my 20-month-old daughter is home with me, too. It seems counterintuitive, but because I have to manage taking care of her and keeping her happy and entertained while still getting my work done, the pressure helps to keep me focused. When she's napping or entertaining herself, I go into super-productive work mode."*

Real and external deadlines are typically provided by clients or bosses, which is how Timebenders can make a success of home working, though our tendency to get 80% of the work done in the last 20% of time left before a deadline means that we will often be laboring late into the night, or through the weekend. The lack of clear boundaries means work is always on hand. Mike is a small business adviser who operates from a home office in the small apartment where he lives alone, and has found himself getting increasingly overwhelmed by the lack of separation between his work and his home life. He works from his dining table, in the same room where he watches tv and eats his meals. Each evening after his dinner he has to decide whether to turn on the tv or carry on working, and work usually wins. *"I'm feeling stressed out because I never seem to stop working. There's always more to do, and I never manage to relax."* Despite the cost, he has decided the solution to hire desk space in a serviced office, in order to regain his work/life balance.

Terry found a perfect solution to this issue: *"My partner and I are both self-employed, and we work from home in a small cabin fitted*

WORKING FROM HOME

out as an office. Because of the insurance, we must double lock the office door and set the alarm overnight. Turning the key in the lock, punching in the alarm code and walking the 30 seconds back to the house means we aren't tempted to return outside office hours. It also means that we have a clear boundary between work and leisure, so the office is just for working, and free of distractions."

There can be positive benefits to working from home if your work requires long periods of concentration. Freelance writers, graphic artists and software designers fall into this category. Provided you have deadlines to motivate you, working from a home office has the benefit of leaving you in peace, once you are "in the flow." Rick is a software designer who uses a concept called a "memory stack" to help himself deal with distractions. The principal behind a memory stack is "first in last out" (FILO), so if he gets distracted, he makes sure he works his way back through the pile until he gets back to the point where he started. For example, he might be busy working when he gets distracted by an email from the bank, telling him his account statement is ready. He clicks on the link in the email to check his balance, and he is asked for his password. He keeps his passwords in a secure file, and when he goes to open it he remembers he wanted to check on an eBay bid etc., etc. In software these are called sub-routines, which are loops within loops. *"It's really important to work backwards carefully until you reach the point where you took the first detour. If you want to avoid 'stack overflow' you have to move some of the stuff to medium term storage,"* he explains. In real life, this means that if he gets too many distractions, he writes them on a list and deals with them later.

Top Tips for Working from Home

- ▶ Always Ask for a Deadline (Deadline Tip 1)

- ▶ Make a Ulysses Contract (Deadline Tip 5)

- ▶ Always Have an Untidy Desk (Distraction Tip 1)

- ▶ Start Early (Distraction Tip 5)

- ▶ Beware the Voodoo Power of Lists (Distraction Tip 8)

- ▶ Calm Your Inner Rebel (Distraction Tip 9)

- ▶ Beware Bad Habits (Distraction Tip 10)

Good Careers for Timebenders

Timebending is such a daily struggle that it is worth trying to find a career in which you're not endlessly fighting your demons. We can work in any field that we choose, but some jobs are better structured for Timebending tendencies, and fit our strengths rather than our weaknesses.

I've come for the Time Management job

We have an advantage in professions which require bursts of intense activity, with a fixed finishing point. We are less likely to enjoy repetitive work; where we need to follow a strict routine; and where there are no milestones or endpoints. We enjoy the adrenaline rush when a job is urgent, and we are better than most at getting projects completed if we have clear deadlines. Work that is structured around short timescales keeps us motivated and stimulated, and helps us to focus on getting things finished. The discipline of having to overcome our closure anxiety on a regular basis helps us to feel in control during our working hours, and may rub off into our personal sphere.

There are many jobs that fit our preferences – too many to name – but here is a list of careers which Timebenders have enjoyed:

o Academic

o Actor

o Hairdresser

o Business consultant

o Counsellor

o Creative agency executive

o Detective

o Doctor

o Journalist

o Osteopath

o Paramedic

o Personal trainer

o Reporter

o Sales representative

o Teacher

o Therapist

o Veterinarian

The jobs we all know we should avoid are those with a regular routine, where there are few interruptions. Bookkeeper, administrator, research scientist and data entry clerk are examples of careers which Timebenders do not usually enjoy. We would tend to get distracted, and then get the work finished in a rush at the end of the day – not quite what the boss is looking for.

Retirement

Timebenders benefit from the structure and deadlines of work routines, and it's not until retirement that underlying problems with closure become more apparent. Once we lose this discipline, we can struggle to complete anything. Without the daily grind we no longer have a deadline for getting up, getting dressed or having breakfast, and we don't need to get to bed by a certain time either. This is when Parkinson's Law "*Work expands to fill the time available,*" really comes into its own. Without the constant pressure of deadlines, everything takes us longer, and we soon find ourselves saying, "*I don't know how I ever found the time to go to work!*"

Retirement is now a two-stage process. In the past, pensioners were usually worn out and in poor health, so an unproductive day might have been welcomed, but nowadays retirees are usually still fit and active, despite the rise in state pension age. Timebenders know that they benefit from staying busy and socially connected, and if they aren't in paid work, they can find volunteering opportunities.

Newly retired Timebenders can find their days filling up so fast that they are soon busier than when they were at work. Some are trapped in a double-decker sandwich, dividing their time between looking after their ageing parents and also providing childcare for their grandchildren. If you don't have family ties, you can still be in demand "*Now you've retired, could you help us with…?*" The opportunities are endless – volunteering; leisure

classes; online learning; joining a choir; taking up art or bridge or golf or gardening. As a Timebender, just make sure you think before plunging in, as once we start something, it's not so easy to stop.

The struggle with lateness doesn't change, no matter how much time we now have to get ready. Debbie gives an example: *"I'll be 69 in a couple of weeks, and I've been 15 minutes late since I was five, when kindergarten demanded I be there on time. I recently sent myself into atrial fibrillation when I couldn't find a parking place for a doctor's appointment and had to walk briskly for two blocks. Was*

I on time for the next appointment? Only because the clinic pads appointment times by 15 minutes."

Living with a Timekeeper can be a real bonus in retirement, because our partners can lay down the markers which help to give us structure. However, this can create tensions as well. When two people start spending 24 hours a day in each other's company, the differences between them become much more obvious, and accusations can start to fly. It's definitely time to make changes if you hope to survive the next thirty years together. There are no easy answers, but here is how one couple found an understanding of Timebending could help resolve their differences.

Jane and Tim had been together for 20 years, but it wasn't until they retired that their opposing attitudes to closure became apparent. Tim loved having lots to do, and enthusiastically took on the job of maintaining their large timber house in New Jersey, which was in endless need of painting and repair. Tim also had shared ownership in a lakeside cabin, together with his siblings, where he also carried out the maintenance. Jane liked to get tasks finished, and was getting increasingly upset as she looked around at the rotting woodwork, unfinished painting and faulty electrical wiring in their beautiful home. It looked so bad she was embarrassed to invite friends over. She couldn't understand why Tim was spending so much time at the lake cabin, carrying out work that was less urgent, and anyway could be done by a local handyman. It wasn't until she learned the power of deadlines that she finally understood – Tim was working at the lake house because the public water supply was cut off at the end of October, when the cold weather made the place uninhabitable. Tim was enjoying the challenge of meeting this target. Their main home had become an endless task, where he drifted between jobs with no sense of purpose. Jane solved the problem by creating real and external deadlines at their home, through planning family gatherings and inviting people to stay, and in short bursts of enthusiasm Tim was finally able to get most of the maintenance finished.

Lone Timebending

Timebenders need external deadlines to get going, which can be a real challenge if we live on our own, once we no longer have the structure provided by employment. As we know only too well, if we don't have deadlines, we tend to dither. Even though we might wake up thinking that we will get some exercise, mow the lawn, or start sorting out the attic, we can easily end up not getting around to doing any of these things, or else finally make it into the attic at midnight, since bed is the only real deadline in our day (even if it's 2am). This has been made harder now that the tv schedules no longer divide up our day, and the network never closes down. If we turn on the tv first thing in the morning, we can get hooked on watching the rolling news for hours. We can find ourselves floating in time and space, and achieving very little, if we have no external deadlines at all.

There are so many distractions waiting to tempt us that we can drift from one thing to another, losing our sense of reality. Self-discipline can ebb away and, whatever our weakness, someone is ready to make money out of us. On-line gambling, shopping and porn are great time wasters, and eating, smoking and drinking help to distract us. Exercise costs nothing and is good for us, but because it takes a bit more effort, it can be the one thing that we never quite get around to. Lack of structure and stimulation can lead to episodes of depression. To avoid sinking into lethargy, Extrovert Timebenders need to keep their calendars full, and avoid having too many flat and empty days. At the other extreme, Introvert Timebenders need to avoid getting lost in their internal world, or they can have difficulty carrying out normal everyday tasks like cooking and shopping.

As ever, the main goal is to find activities that have deadlines. There are clubs and classes to suit all tastes, either for physical exercise or stimulating the mind, but avoid on-line learning, unless the course is structured in real time. In case this is sounding too disheartening, there are plenty of solutions if you look for them. Andrea finally decided to divorce her husband once her son had left university, which meant that she went solo just around the time she retired. She was nervous about living alone, as her energy came from being with people. As part of her plan she signed up for the daily 9am class at her local gym, which was a great way of getting herself up and dressed and out of the house. She also found a new companion, a wonderful dog called Poppy which required regular walking and feeding, and gave her all the affection she needed. Looking after a pet is an ideal way to bring structure into your life if you live alone, because they need regular feeding and exercise, as well as social contact.

And if we follow all this advice, and live long enough, we might end up in Long-Term Care, where our days will be structured by routines, and we will soon start complaining about all the rules!

Top Tips for Retirement

▶ Involve Other People (Deadline Tip 2)

▶ Start with the Fun Stuff and Do the Work Later (Distraction Tip 2)

▶ Give Yourself a Double Bind (Distraction Tip 3)

▶ Look for the Carrots (Distraction Tip 4)

PART FOUR

Delving Deeper

Why Do We Do It?

"Hurrying and delaying are alike ways of trying to resist the present."

ALAN WATTS, PHILOSOPHER

Having admitted how crazy life can be for a Timebender, we have to ask ourselves what is going on? Why are we making life so uncomfortable for ourselves? Why can't we just do what we say we will do? Why are our lives such an internal tussle?

Let's start with a health warning. Although 20% of the population struggle with punctuality, there is a subset within this group whose behavior is extreme. The inability to focus, transition, or complete tasks can be linked to an underlying condition such as depression, Asperger Syndrome or ADD/ADHD. If you think you, or someone you know, falls into this category, there are treatments available, and it would be advisable to seek professional help. But if we believe our behavior falls within the "normal" range, we must still recognize that it causes inconvenience to ourselves and distress to our loved ones, so why don't we change? There has to be a hidden benefit, or we wouldn't do it. What's the payoff for us? Every bad habit has its reward, but what can that possibly be?

After a lifetime of Timebending, I have come up with three possibilities:

1. We work best under pressure. Might we unconsciously be aware that our thinking process actually improves when our adrenaline kicks in?

2. We love the adrenaline rush. We are hooked on that buzz of fear. It is our own personal white-knuckle ride, which makes us feel alive.

3. This behavior is an unconscious rebellion, stemming from our childhood, when we were forced to conform to other people's demands. Now that we are adults we are still resisting. We know what we "should" be doing, but the five-year-old inside us is stamping its little feet and refusing to obey.

I have no definitive answers, so let's explore these three options together. These factors may work separately, or they may overlap, depending on the situation. I hope that this will just be the beginning of the investigation, and that others will bring their research and expertise to take the subject to a new level.

Let's look at each possibility in turn.

Do We Work Better Under Pressure?

C ould it be that some mix of neurotransmitters released in our brains just before a deadline improves our functioning? Maybe deadlines don't just force us to get the job finished – they help us to perform certain tasks better. Might we have more imaginative ideas when our pulses are racing? Do the connections in our brains spark off each other in new ways?

There are numerous examples of outstanding work achieved under pressure. Martin Luther King famously added the words *"I have a dream"* to his speech just as he was standing up to make his address. Spike Milligan, Douglas Adams, Lewis Carroll, Aaron Sorkin, Jennifer Saunders and Helen Fielding were all ground breakers. Did they unconsciously realize that the last minute was when they did their best work? Is it a coincidence that the best comic geniuses seem to have the worst reputation for this?

Improv comedians walk out on stage without knowing what they are going to say – yet they often seem to get more laughter from the audience than stand ups who have prepared their scripts well in advance. Is the adrenaline making them funnier? It isn't just the famous who do this. Wannabe comedian Audrey told me that when she put her name forward to do her first stand-up comedy routine at her local club, she didn't decide what she was going to say until half an hour before the performance. She let a few ideas mull around in her head during the days beforehand, but she brought everything together at the last minute. She might have just needed the deadline to get down to it, but maybe it wasn't just about being able to concentrate – did she instinctively know she would be more creative?

Neuroscience is uncovering new insights into the way our brains trigger our behavior and may have already come up with some answers. We now know that our "fight, flight or freeze" response comes from the amygdala. If it detects a threat, it secretes the neurochemicals dopamine and serotonin in our brains, and hormones such as adrenaline and cortisol in our bodies. Joseph LeDoux, an American neuroscientist based at the Department of Psychology at New York University, and a specialist in the area of fear and anxiety, explains that "*attention, perception, memory and arousal*" are stimulated by the amygdala when we feel stressed, and that these "*coalesce in consciousness and compel one to feel fear.*" Could it be possible that raised attention, perception and memory also contribute to heightened creativity? Do fear and inspiration go hand in hand?

Charles Limb, Professor at Johns Hopkins School of Medicine, specializes in studying the creative brain, though he believes that it will take another 20 years to understand this fully. Showing great creativity himself, he has found a way of carrying out MRI brain scans on improvising jazz musicians and rap artists while they are performing – getting them to play and improvise while lying horizontal in a scanning tunnel is an impressive achievement. He discovered that, when improvisation is in full flow, the brain turns off the areas linked to self-monitoring and inhibition. At the same time, the brain regions involved with all the senses light up, indicating a heightened state of awareness— the performers literally taste, smell, and feel the air around them.

So perhaps the heightened awareness we Timebenders experience when we are looking into the lion's mouth of an imminent deadline actually improves our creativity. Maybe there is some logic behind our madness, and at some point in the future, the world will decide that Timebenders had it right all along.

Are We Hooked?

"Time flies like an arrow. Fruit flies like a banana."
GROUCHO MARX, COMEDIAN

If we are to unwrap the hidden benefits that keep us trapped in our lateness habit, then it can be helpful to try and break our behavior down into its component parts. There are at least three different stages we go through when we are late, and each trigger their own neurochemicals. Are we late because we are hooked on adrenaline and dopamine? Let's see if we can unravel what is going on in our bodies.

Stage 1. The Starting Pistol (Adrenaline)

The lateness starts long before we might realize. The behavior pattern begins when we fail to stop what we are doing, in order to start getting ready. We suppress our awareness, until we suddenly hit the panic button when we realize we will be late. The panic releases a flood of adrenaline, which increases our heart rate and our blood pressure, and speeds up the blood flow to our larger mus-

OMG! Is that the time?

cles. We start to breathe faster and take in more oxygen. This surge of energy is exhilarating and makes us feel alive. Adrenaline is a real antidote to boredom and stagnation, and feels so good that people can spend large amounts of money to achieve it, by bungee jumping, motor racing and other dangerous sports. Timebenders are achieving it several times a day, just by putting themselves in danger of being late – and all for free.

Stage 2. The Rush to get Ready (Adrenaline and Dopamine)

The rush towards the deadline may involve physical activity, such as racing around the house or running for a train, or it might just need our fingers to tap on a keyboard while our brain focuses on completing a task. Either way, the flow of adrenaline released by the starting pistol continues to pump, giving us a buzz of energy. In addition, when the body is stressed, it also releases dopamine, which is one of the neurotransmitters that controls our mental and emotional responses, as well as our motor reactions. Perhaps it is the dopamine release that enables us to focus our concentration and work more effectively under pressure than other people. We will have to leave it to the neuroscientists to find out.

Stage 3. The Finishing Line (Dopamine)

The primary function of dopamine, which is known as the "happiness hormone," is to flood the pleasure centers of our brain with euphoria when we have achieved a goal. This is how learning is reinforced. When we succeed in arriving on time at our destination, we are rewarded by a surge of elation which is triggered by dopamine.

But hold on a minute – if being on time makes us happy, why don't we seek this reward by always being punctual? The intriguing answer is that, when the result becomes predictable, the level of dopamine diminishes. Recent experiments involving rats implanted with electrodes have shown this happening real-time, but these results just confirmed the conclusions reached by American psychologists Ferster and Skinner back in 1957, before MRI scanners existed. They put rats in a box and trained them to press levers to produce a pellet of food. To their surprise, they found that the strongest way to reinforce learned behavior in rats is to reward them intermittently, and it turns out that humans behave in the same way. We lose interest when something is totally predictable, but we are compulsively attracted to random rewards. The shot of dopamine diminishes if we succeed every time, but it gets stronger and more enslaving when success only happens occasionally.

Are We Gambling Addicts?

Gambling casino operators deliberately design unpredictable reward systems into their slot machines to trap players into addiction, and videogame designers employ the same techniques. This perhaps explains why anglers will sit silently from dawn to dusk, in rain and mud, in the hope of catching a big fish. This also possibly explains the addictive qualities of Facebook and Instagram – when people feel compelled to keep checking in case someone has responded to their post.

So maybe the state of anxiety we get into when we are hurrying to an appointment, and willing all the lights to be green, is the same state that a gambler at a slot machine experiences as he hopes for a big win. When we manage to arrive on time, the exhilaration we feel is comparable to the gaming addict who hears the coins come tumbling out of the slot. Pepperice, who fights hard to overcome her Timebending habit, knows the feeling very well: *"I get a little secret proud thrill if I managed to leave at the last possible minute and arrive exactly on time. Because it's like I beat time. I BEAT TIME."* And it's not just about winning. Gamblers know that they get a buzz from the act of gambling, even if they don't win. Mark Griffiths, a psychologist at Nottingham Trent University who specializes in behavioral addictions, surveyed 5,500 gamblers to understand their motivation. The chance to *"win big money"* was the strongest factor, but it was followed closely by *"because it's exciting."* It all comes down to the neurochemicals. *"Even when you're losing while you're gambling, your body is still producing adrenalin and endorphins,"* Mark explains. *"People are buying entertainment."*

Not only are we addicted to intermittent rewards, but research shows the appeal is even stronger if we think we ALMOST achieved a win. This knowledge is like gold dust to casino operators. One-armed bandit designers have learned that if they make the third matching fruit come to a stop where it ALMOST lines up with the other two, the gambler is more motivated to keep playing, because he imagines that he is within a hair's breadth of winning. Near misses mistakenly lead a gambler to believe he wins more than he loses. For Timebenders, a near miss would be turning up just as an event is starting, and sliding into a seat without attracting attention. We imagine we have beaten the clock, and feel not only the exhilaration of the adrenaline, but also win the reward of the dopamine hit which comes with success. This also explains why, unless we keep an accurate record, we can believe that we are nearly always on time.

This is backed up by a 2009 study by researchers from the University of Stanford in California, who found that the fact that people lost money when visiting a casino did not necessarily impact their overall enjoyment of the experience. The stress of the situation raises the adrenaline levels and creates a feeling of exhilaration which is a reward in itself. In a similar way, a Timebender rushing to an appointment feels alert and alive, even though red lights and slow drivers are causing stress and frustration. So maybe we are getting a gambler's high from the chance of being on time once in a while, and we're actually addicted to the stress of running late? The power of the dopamine system to alter habits is already familiar to drug addicts and smokers. Every habit-forming drug, from amphetamines to cocaine, from nicotine to alcohol, dispenses a shot of dopamine. These drugs take a shortcut straight to the reward center of the brain, avoiding the prefrontal cortex, which normally helps people to control impulsive behavior. The more an addict uses a drug, the harder it becomes to stop.

The Demon Deadline Shaver Unmasked

Gambling may also have something to teach us about our crazy habit of shaving our deadlines, which every true Time-bender recognizes, but none of us can control. It is possible to understand our Demon Deadline Shaver (DDS) as a gambling addict, hiding in our subconscious, if you substitute "adrenaline high" in place of cash as the reward. Whenever there is a) a specific deadline and b) a predictable elapsed time period, he seizes his chance to gamble on the outcome. You are the only entrant in this race – he bets against you beating your own best record.

To make the wager work, your DDS needs to wait for the right circumstances – a journey you have done often enough for the time to be predictable, with a deadline at the end. Going to work, or to a class, or taking kids to school, all fit this category. Your DDS then needs to allow you precisely the same period of time as your previous best effort. He will keep distracting you if you try to get ready early, and only fire the starting pistol at the last minute. Your unconscious goal is to beat your own best time. The star prize is the flood of dopamine you will get if you arrive by the deadline, and the consolation prize is the adrenaline high you will win every time, even though you're late. However, if you arrive EARLY, something very strange hap-

160

pens. Your DDS gets out his stopwatch and makes a careful note, and when you next undertake the same competition, he makes sure that he's shaved off those extra minutes before he sets the panic button off.

When people ran their lives by the sun and seasons, rather than by accurate clocks, the Demon Deadline Shaver had no fun at all. To throw him off your shoulder today, you have to take away his toys by avoiding a) a specific deadline, and b) a regular situation where you can predict the time required. It can take some imagination, but here are a few ideas.

o If you are catching a train, avoid looking up the actual time the train will depart. Just find out how frequently they run, and allow enough time to wait for the next one.

o Change your routine on regular journeys, so that you never really get to know your fastest speed. You could maybe stop to post a letter, buy a paper, fill up with fuel, or even vary your route.

o Change your mode of transport – maybe alternate between walking, cycling and driving on short journeys.

Why the Habit is So Hard to Kick

New insights into the functioning of our brain help to explain why lateness is such a hard habit to change. David Zald, Professor of Psychology and Psychiatry at Vanderbilt University in Tennessee, used brain scanning to reveal that there are fewer dopamine-inhibiting receptors in the brains of thrill seekers. Without inhibitors, the brains of these risk takers get more saturated with dopamine than most, which predisposes them to keep chasing the next high. Zald's theory is that people who take risks get an unusually big hit of dopamine each time, because their brains are not able to inhibit the neurotransmitter adequately. That blast makes them feel so good that they keep repeating the behavior.

However, we have more to learn from studying addiction. Over time, brain receptors become overwhelmed, with the result that dopamine has less impact. People who develop an addiction typically find that, over time, the desired substance no longer gives them the same reward — an effect known as tolerance. However, the memory persists, and prompts addicts to keep repeating the experience. Is this why lateness can eventually become a tired old habit that keeps us trapped us in unwanted behavior patterns?

Identifying the cues that prompt the behavior, and avoiding them, are important elements in the battle to overcome compulsive behavior. Environmental or emotional triggers are known to cause people to relapse, which is why rehab can be recommended for addiction recovery. Being isolated from a drug for a period of between 30-90 days allows the body time to detox. Rehab for Timebenders seemed like an impossible concept until the arrival of COVID-19, but when the world went into lockdown, we had a glimpse of how this would feel. Our adrenaline levels fell dramatically once we could no longer go anywhere other than for a stroll in the park. Clicking into an online meeting didn't produce the same buzz as racing to a physical location. Life became calmer, and we had a chance to take a new look at our lives. Whether this period of isolation from the triggers which make us late has given us more control over our behavior has not been tested, but we have at last had an insight into what it must feel like to be calm and in control.

Maybe one day the neuroscientists will come up with a pill that will help us to kick the adrenaline habit? Or maybe there are other ways to reprogram our brains? Could therapy have any answers?

Can Therapy Help?

After struggling with my lateness habit for many years, I eventually decided to look for outside help. I knew that my conscious mind wanted to be on time, but was sabotaged by something I couldn't control, so I wondered whether I could work at a deeper level. Could I solve the problem by persuading my subconscious to be on time? Having studied other people's experiences, I had no confidence that "traditional talk therapy" would make any difference. To quote Erin, *"I've been in years of therapy and 89% of each session starts with a discussion of my tardiness: 'I'm proud, I'm early today!' Therapist: 'Well, you were actually on time not early and let's talk about how you feel right now.' My husband calls it pathological tardiness."*

So what other options are out there? The treatment usually recommended for retraining thoughts and altering behaviors is Cognitive Behavior Therapy (CBT). I liked the idea that CBT teaches practical and helpful strategies that can be incorporated into everyday life. It is the treatment recommended for compulsive behavior such as hoarding and OCD, in combination with anti-anxiety medication. However, on investigation, I couldn't find any convincing case studies that showed that CBT had helped anyone with a lateness problem. I also wasn't sure that my behavior was caused by anxiety or depression, which are assumed to lie beneath unwanted behavior patterns.

However, my searches did uncover people who claimed they had overcome undesirable spontaneous behaviors, such as smoking, overeating and nail biting, through hypnotherapy. I was encouraged when I found that the National Health Service website – a source of unbiased advice – recommends hypnotherapy to change unwanted habits and to relieve pain. I was excited to think that I could stop being late just by having the idea suggested to me while in a trance. I signed up for a course of sessions with a local hypnotherapist, who claimed to be able to fix *"undesirable spontaneous behaviors and bad habits."* He started by asking me an intriguing question – could I visualize my "timeline"? Revealingly, I saw it whizzing into space, somewhere past my right ear. Unfortunately, this was the most relevant question of the entire treatment. It proved to be a waste of money, as he wasn't a Timebender and lacked any understanding of the problem.

Feeling disillusioned, I decided to stick to personal recommendations only. One of my friends suggested I try a course of Emotional Freedom Technique (EFT), which she had used successfully herself. I'd never heard of it, but I was curious, as she said EFT is a tool for *"changing behaviors one has no control over."* I discovered that EFT is also known as tapping, and sometimes described as *"acupuncture without the needles."* It turned out to be a widely-used technique and I soon found a local practitioner. EFT works by exploring feelings and core issues, while gently tapping on seven acupuncture points around the face and shoulders. I was surprised that I'd never come across it before, since I quickly found it remarkably effective. By the end of the second session, my therapist had persuaded me to reset my watch to the correct time – a habit I had been wedded to for 20 years. The reframing suggestion that "*Time is your friend, not your enemy*" came as a shock, because it revealed to me that I had been fighting time all my life. I worked on freeing myself from negative emotions, which included childhood guilt and rebellion against parental authority, and began to focus on listening to my own needs. The EFT sessions gave me tools that I have continued to use ever since. If I feel myself sliding into that familiar panic about wanting to be early, but knowing I will make myself late, I can calm myself with tapping. Once I am calm, I can make more rational choices. The explanation of how tapping works is slowly being revealed through the advances of neuroscience. The latest theory is that tapping on the body's energy meridians interrupts the signal to the cortex, which stops the panicky thought from going straight to the "fight, flight or freeze" amygdala, and gives it time to reroute via the rational frontal lobes. It has gained a reputation as one of the few therapies effective in treating trauma and PTSD.

I knew I hadn't given hypnosis a fair chance, but I needed to find a therapist who could relate to my problem. I managed to book a single hypnotherapy session with a practitioner who was herself a Timebender, and whose approach was far more helpful. She focused on my aversion to being early. She put me into a light trance and had me visualize myself getting dressed and ready to leave the house for my exercise class in a calm and orderly way. When I could see myself standing by my back door with my coat on, with time to spare, she encouraged me to savor the feeling of stepping through the door without any sense of anxiety, and closing it behind me. She then had me visualize my early arrival at the class and explore the positive feelings it gave me. This single session has helped me to push through the moment of closure, and to resist the urge to go back and change my shoes.

Am I cured? It would be more accurate to say that I am "in recovery." I now understand why I am late, and what the key triggers are. I feel more in control of my behavior because I can see what I am doing and why I am doing it. I am no longer in denial, and I am more aware of the impact my lateness has on other people – especially if they are at the opposite end of the scale to me. This doesn't mean that I am always early, but I am less likely to be late.

Martin Seligman, the renowned American psychologist, questions whether therapeutic intervention can ever truly change us, in his book "What You Can Change ... And What You Can't." He concludes that *"most psychological symptoms stem from heritable personality traits that can be ameliorated but not wholly eliminated."* However, as the father of "positive psychology," he gives us his own solution – what we need is *"courage to understand our psychological problems and manage them so as to function well in spite of them."*

I agree with Martin – I don't believe I can completely eliminate my lateness habit. As Jung identified, my aversion to closure is hardwired into my psyche. In the same way that an Introvert cannot turn themselves into an Extrovert, I will never develop a preference for getting things finished and out of the way. However, by becoming aware of my behavior patterns, I can choose to go against my natural preferences. I can be on time when I need to be. When relaxed, however, I will always revert to type, so sadly I will still be a little late when meeting my loved ones.

PART FIVE

Guidelines for Partners

The Nightmare of Living with a Timebender

L et's face it – living with a Timebender is a nightmare. We use our partners as our adrenaline trigger – when they start to explode, we know it is time to get moving. This is really unfair on them, very bad for their health, and possibly the biggest problem in our relationship.

Being ready on time must seem like such a simple thing to ask of us – yet we just can't do it. It looks like we just don't care about their feelings. Why are we never ready until they get annoyed? They can't believe that we have no control over our behavior. They might struggle with punctuality themselves, but if they are always waiting for us, it means that they have found their own ways of dealing with the problem.

Our poor partners try their best to find ways of improving our timekeeping, but sometimes they achieve exactly the opposite. The classic spouse's solution is to add a margin onto any deadline they give us. This works the first time, but they have taken the first step down a very slippery slope, as a deadline has to be real. Once we realize they have fudged a start time, we will assume they always do it, and we will therefore get later. They will then add a bigger margin – which is where the slippery slope comes in.

The good news is that partners can make a big difference if they understand a few basic guidelines. It is best to come clean, acknowledge our problems with lateness, and ask for their help.

Guidelines for Living with a Timebender

1. Always Give Us a Deadline (with Consequences)

If you need us to accomplish a task, always tell us when it is needed by, and give us real consequences if we fail. Avoid telling us a job isn't urgent, because we will probably never get around to doing it.

2. Don't Tell Us What to Do

Don't tell us what we "must do," because this will create a real obstacle to it ever getting done. Don't write lists of tasks for us, for the same reason.

3. Make Us Set Our Own Deadlines

If you need us to get somewhere on time, get us to take control. Provide us with all the information we need about estimated journey times; likely traffic; event start time etc. and then ask us when we think we must be ready. You could remind us to add on the transition time we need to allow for putting on coats and shoes and finding keys.

Lateness begins when we fail to allow enough time to *start* getting ready, so ask us to calculate this starting point as well. If you can tactfully remind us, when this moment is approaching, we may not thank you, but deep down we will be grateful.

4. Try Not to Get Mad

If you lose your temper every time a deadline goes whooshing by, then this becomes our way of assessing how late we are. We will use your tolerance limit as our starting pistol. Once the steam starts to come out of your ears, we will decide it is time to stop dithering and get a move on. This is not good for either of us, so see if you can find other ways in which you can convince us that time is up.

5. Don't Give an Inch

We need you to be cruel to be kind, in order to show us that the deadlines are genuine. Our adrenaline is triggered by fear – so give us something to be afraid of, other than your anger. If you need to get somewhere at a certain time, and we aren't ready, leave without us. (I can't believe I am writing this!) Once you have done this, we will take your deadlines seriously. Tell us what time we need to leave – and stick to it.

Hopefully you won't have to do this more than once, to convince us you mean business. It would be best if you can choose an occasion when we could follow you in a taxi, or when it doesn't matter if we don't turn up. We will, of course, be really annoyed, but that will at least redress the balance a bit.

6. Give Us a Starting Signal

Some sort of countdown is incredibly helpful – like those theatre announcements that say, "*The performance will be starting in five minutes.*" In those last minutes, our Timebending superpower will kick in and we will race to the deadline. Ringing a bell to give a five-minute warning of your impending departure might seem a bit over the top, but it would trigger our adrenaline and get us moving like one of Pavlov's dogs. Opening the front door, or starting the car engine, and then leaving soon after the agreed deadline is also very effective.

My gold medal award goes to Steven, who started to learn to play the piano at around the same time as he married his Timebending wife Kate. As a deadline approached, once he was ready and waiting, he would sit down at the piano and start practicing. As soon as she heard the tinkling of piano keys, Kate knew that she'd better get a move on. Instead of getting cross, he improved his piano playing.

There may be ways you could adapt this in your household, perhaps by starting to prime the burglar alarm, or locking the windows? Any signal to our subconscious is useful, even if you decide to blast out loud music five minutes before it is time to leave.

7. Always Allow Us an Unspoken Margin

We aren't good at measuring time, we tend to forget about the "transition time" needed to put on coats and find keys, and we always squeeze our deadlines on regular journeys. As a result, we will always be a little bit late. It is an inner compulsion we struggle to control. If you ask us to **admit** that we are going to be five minutes late, we will simply adopt this as our new deadline, and be ready five minutes after that. So please just factor in an extra five minutes to every deadline you give us, without asking us to acknowledge it.

8. Don't Lie to Us About Starting Times

Telling us an important event will start earlier than it does can appears to be a good strategy, but it can be counterproductive. Mistakenly believing that an event begins half an hour earlier than it does will initially succeed in making us early, but if you repeat the deception we will assume you will always lie, and we will factor this in, and end up being later than before. A deadline has to be real and have consequences, if it is to trigger our adrenaline. It is more helpful if you give us incontrovertible facts. For example, we might be quite shocked if you showed us

172

a record of the time we said we would be ready and the actual time we arrived, during the past month.

9. Give Us an Incentive

Since we are probably late because we subconsciously enjoy the adrenaline kick, consider whether you can give us an alternative reward. **Betting** that we will be late will give us an incentive to be on time – provided you can wager something that motivates us. The forfeit might be that we will have to take on an unpleasant chore if we lose, or that we will be let off one if we win. Whatever the bet, you must enforce the outcome. Alternatively, you could simply **challenge** us to be on time, making it clear that you don't believe we can do it. This can motivate us to rebel against your negative view. Another approach would be to create a **competition** around being on time, which can work well with children.

10. Don't Bottle It Up

It is important that you show us how difficult you find our lack of punctuality. If you try to conceal your feelings, there is a chance we won't realize how our behavior impacts you, and we might mistake your calmness for acceptance. Most of us are in denial about our lateness and bury any awareness of how our actions affect other people. It helps if we feel a jolt of guilt about keeping you waiting, because that is what gets us moving. Fear and guilt trigger our adrenaline, which is the force that gets us rushing around and out of the door. Once we know you're upset, we should be bringing you higher up our Secret Scale of Acceptable Lateness.

11. Please Don't Take It Personally

We are battling with unconscious drives, and we don't deliberately choose to be late. While our behavior is very inconsiderate, we never intend to make your life difficult. You are extremely important to us, in our battle with timekeeping – though we will probably never tell you this. We really value you and don't want to drive you away, in spite of appearances. If you can help us to reduce our lateness habit, we would be eternally grateful.

12. Try to See the Positive Side

We know that our Timebending can be a nightmare for you, but there might possibly be a few benefits that come with the package. We can be very adaptable and flexible; we will often drop what we are doing if you ask for our help; we can achieve miracles when time is short; and we can stay calm when everything seems to be going haywire. Although we might be very different to you, together we make a good combination.

How to Stay Friends with a Timebender

We are usually attracted to people who are similar to us, and this is as true for our attitudes to timekeeping as our taste in music or films. Punctuality is a trait that slowly reveals itself over time and will not be obvious at the beginning of a friendship.

Once an early bird realizes that they are repeatedly being kept waiting, they can become upset enough to distance themselves from Timebending friends. Timebenders, on the other hand, will probably be unaware of the effect they are having, and will be most surprised if they ever learn the truth. They will feel very comfortable, however, with friends who are as late as they are, which tends to draw them towards other Timebenders.

If you are attracted to a Timebender in spite of their poor punctuality, you might like some guidelines on how to avoid the key triggers for conflict in your relationship.

1. Make your own travel arrangements whenever possible. If you must share a car journey, make sure you are the driver, and be very clear about the time you will arrive to pick them up. (Always factor in 5-10 minutes for them to change their shoes, find their bag and feed the cat).

2. Keep control of your own tickets. Never rely on your friend to get you onto a train or plane. Always arrange to meet in your seat in a theatre or concert hall. If you agree to meet up outside, you might both miss the start.

3. If you are meeting in a park, café or restaurant, have something to keep you busy while you wait. Smartphones and eBooks are a great help here. If you are absorbed in reading, you won't have wasted your time, which will help you not to feel resentful or get agitated. Best to feel surprised when they arrive.

4. Call when someone is so late that you begin to worry. You will probably have to leave a message, but it makes the point. Call again if you need to.

5. Tell them how you feel. If you keep your feelings hidden, they will not know you are upset.

6. Try not to take it personally. They are struggling to control their compulsive behavior. They don't do it deliberately, or because they think their time is more important than yours. They just don't have your ability to leave the house on time.

7. If you want to understand what they are going through, try to imagine how it would feel to force yourself to be late. The anxiety you would be feeling is similar in some ways to the anxiety they feel about trying to arrive early. It is illogical, but nevertheless very real.

8. If their lateness is getting worse, and really bugging you, then you will only resolve the situation by making the deadline real and with consequences – in

other words, you have to leave without them. It sounds harsh, but it is the only way to reverse the trend. Your friendship is suffering anyway, so it is worth risking drastic action in order to save it.

Here are two contrasting approaches showing how it is possible to stay friends with a Timebender.

Kate:

"I'm a fairly punctual person who is friends with someone who is chronically late. Early on in our friendship it was really angering being kept waiting all the time. But I've learned to anticipate the half an hour time difference he seems to be on. If I'm meeting him somewhere, I will show up half an hour late. If he's my ride somewhere, I tell him we have to be there half an hour before we do. It seemed like a mean thing to do to him when I first started, since there was always the potential of him being 'on time,' which would actually make him half an hour early. But the one or two times that's actually happened he's usually so relieved because he's never early for things!

"But the bottom line is I really value this friend and accept that this is a flaw he has. And I'm not a perfect person or friend either and he still values me. Obviously I want him to keep trying to be more punctual – as any friend supports another when they're working on their self-improvement – but being cross with him constantly isn't going to fix it."

Spencer:

"I had a roommate / best friend who was always late. In the beginning of our friendship, I would wait stupid amounts of time for him to get his shit together. Later on in our friendship I realized I was indirectly condoning his behavior by waiting for him. So instead of getting frustrated, I would just carry on without him. What surprised me was that he acted as though no one had ever just left without him before, like it was a brand-new concept to him that people wouldn't just sit around waiting for him."

Guidelines for Partners – Summary

► Always Give Us a Deadline (with Consequences)

► Don't Tell Us What to Do

► Make Us Set Our Own Deadlines

► Don't Give an Inch

► Try Not to Get Mad

► Give Us a Starting Signal

► Always Allow Us an Unspoken Margin

► Don't Lie to Us About Starting Times

► Give Us an Incentive

► Don't Bottle It Up

► Please Don't Take It Personally

► Try to See the Positive Side

PART SIX

The Timebender's Workbook

What Next for Timebenders?

So, you've almost finished this book, and are just about to move on to your next activity. Has anything changed as a result of your reading? You hopefully have more awareness of the behaviors which make you late, and when they show up in your life. You might now be able to anticipate the moments which used to take you by surprise – not being ready when your guests arrive; getting stressed about leaving for your vacation; getting distracted when you have a big task to complete. You also have some tools to trick yourself into being on time. But if you would really like to free yourself from scampering around in your endless hamster-wheel of stress and anxiety, then it might take a little longer.

Awareness is half the battle, but to break a habit, you need to re-educate your subconscious mind, and this doesn't happen by just skimming through a book. You need to change your pattern of behavior for at least 21 days if you want to program your brain to start making different choices. This can be tough, and most readers will quietly fade away at this point. If you decide that you are serious about achieving change, then you need to devote time to carrying out some exercises.

If you are disciplined enough to work on this alone, then you are an unusual Timebender. For the rest of us, the best way to start is by finding an ally. Engaging a therapist or Life Coach could be a very good move, because if you are spending money, you will be extra motivated to get results. Alternatively, enlist a friend who understands and can support you. You might even be able to start a group, along the lines of Weight Watchers. If you have a loving and supportive partner who will help you without judgement or criticism, then you are very fortunate in being able to ask for their backing.

If you want to find supportive buddies online, then check out my website at www.timebending.co.uk or join our Not Late but Timebending group on Facebook, or contact me on Twitter – Grace G Pacie (@OnlyTimebending).

You might want to buy yourself a workbook – something small enough to carry around. This will be where you keep a record of your punctuality and will be where you can recognize your achievements. If you prefer, you can use your smartphone or tablet. If you want to share, then start a blog. Whichever way you decide do it, the following pages provide you with the activities that will allow you to start forming new habits and moving away from old unwanted behaviors. You will, of course, need a real and external deadline to carry these out, so you'll need to arrange to check in with your buddy/therapist/group at the end of the time period. An ideal plan would be to take a week for each exercise, but you can take longer if that works better for you. Tackle each one at a time – don't overlap.

Let's start with getting that Demon Deadline Shaver off our backs.

Exercise 1

How to Beat the Demon Deadline Shaver –
A 10 Step Guide

The Demon Deadline Shaver is an adrenaline addict, which is why he will always delay you from getting moving until time is short. The way to beat him is to start to get ready in good time, and not wait until he hits the panic button.

This approach can be applied to any deadline you really don't want to miss. It also works well if you are habitually late for something and need to reprogram an unrealistic expectation of the journey time. Let's assume, for this example, that you want to ensure you will leave home at a certain time. This is what to do:

1. Well in advance, when you are calm, work out what time you will need to start your journey to get to your destination in good time. If you use a navigation app to make this calculation, add another 5% or 10%.

2. Find a blank sheet of paper and at the bottom of the page write the time you will need to leave. **(a)**

3. Now go to the top of the page and list all the tasks you will need to carry out before you will be ready to

leave, together with an estimate of how long each will take. Take the time to make a mental picture of yourself carrying out the task. Be as realistic as possible. **(b)**

4. Add on at least five minutes "transition time" to get yourself out of the door – more if needed. **(c)**

5. Add up the figures to discover the total amount of time needed to get ready.

6. Now subtract this from the time at the bottom of your page, to calculate what time you need to start your preparations. Write this, large and bold, at the top of your sheet. **(d)**

7. Take a moment to let this information sink in, and test whether you honestly believe the time you have written down. If you secretly think you have built in a margin of error, remove it and adjust the top figure.

8. Say aloud, with conviction, three times "I will start getting ready at x o'clock." Leave the piece of paper visible.

9. Then put an alert on your phone, or set an alarm, to warn you when you will need to start your preparations. **(e)**

10. When the alarm sounds, DO NOT LET YOURSELF LOOK AT THE TIME, until you have left home and actually closed the door behind you.

What you need to do	Sequence	Time
Set your alarm	**(e)**	7:07am
Calculate starting time and say it aloud	**(d)**	
Measure time needed to get washed and dressed	**(b)**	25 mins
Measure time needed to eat breakfast		15 mins
Measure time needed to get papers ready and pack bag		8 mins
Add transition time	**(c)**	5 mins
Decide what time you need to leave home	**(a)**	8:00am

Exercise 2

Your Own Secret Scale of Acceptable Lateness

Take four pages in your workbook and write the following four headings at the top.

A. Events I can be early for

B. Events I usually manage to be in time for

C. Events I intend to be in time for, but usually arrive late

D. Events I don't think I need to be on time for

Allocate each of the regular activities in your everyday life to one of the four pages.

Alongside the repeat activities or events, write down the names of people who you regularly meet there, and whose opinion matters to you. Take a moment to see your behavior through their eyes.

Look at the list in box C. Jot down next to each event any ideas you have about how you could motivate yourself to arrive early.

o Could you offer someone a lift?

o Do you have a friend who is going to the same event, who you could arrange to meet with before it starts?

o Could you plan to do something non-essential before the event starts, which you could drop like a lizard's tail if you haven't left enough time?

Make a note of the actions you plan to take.

Keep a record in your workbook every time you have a positive result.

Exercise 3

Check Out the Opposition

Think of which key people in your life are Timekeepers. (You are looking for the people who always ready ahead of time, and who are uncomfortable when others are not punctual.)

Write down their names and underneath each write down the advantages and disadvantages that Timekeeping brings to their lives.

In what way do your lives overlap? Make a note of the times they will have been inconvenienced by your Timebending. When has your life been impacted by their Timekeeping?

If you were more in control of time, what impact might this have on your relationship?

If you are feeling brave, and determined to change your ways, share your conclusions with each of these people, and ask for their feedback.

Exercise 4

Measuring Time

1. Measure how long it takes you to get ready for the day. Timebenders find this a very difficult thing to do, so it could be useful to enlist the help of someone you live with to carry out this exercise. This will help you to focus on the task, and not get distracted.

Break your activities into smaller units:

o Taking a shower (how many minutes do you run the water?)

o Cleaning your teeth

o Getting dressed

o Eating your breakfast

2. Repeat the exercise on two other days. Were there any differences? If so, what was the reason for the difference?

3. Measure how much "transition time" it takes you to get out of the door.

4. Calculate how much time you need in total, if you were to get ready without having an adrenaline rush.

You may be reluctant to try this idea because, once you know how long things take, you might be afraid that your Demon Deadline Shaver will squeeze down the time you allow. The truth is exactly the opposite – Timebenders tend to underestimate time by up to 35%, so by measuring your activities you should end up allowing yourself more time, rather than less.

Exercise 5

Check in To Your Feelings –
Check Out Your Closure Anxiety

We're all in denial, but maybe you could be one of those people who is prepared to see through our habit of self-justification? You can do this by listening to your body. Your body registers your feelings, even if your mind is pushing the awareness away.

- o Start by writing down, on a scale of 1-10, how much you believe that you experience Closure Anxiety?

- o Stick a sheet of paper on the inside of the door you use to exit your home and leave a pen handy.

- Whenever you leave the house and close the door behind you in the next week, make a note of what you have done in the final 5-10 minutes before leaving. If you are in too much of a rush to write on the sheet of paper, then make a mental note and jot it down as soon as you can. Then put a tick by all those which you consider were essential.

- At the end of the week, look at what is on the list. Were the things you have ticked really essential? Did they absolutely have to be done before you left home?

The next week, keep a similar list. Do you see any changes in your behavior? On a scale of 1-10, how much do you now believe that you experience Closure Anxiety?

Exercise 6

Moment of Truth

Write a list of all the events you will be attending in the coming week. Next to each, make a note of the time you intend to arrive.

During the week, keep a record of your actual arrival time. No fudging – this isn't the time you rush through the door – this is the moment when you are calm and ready to begin.

In your notebook, write down every excuse you give for being late.

- o How true was it?
- o Give it a truthfulness score out of 10.

Make a resolution to be 100% truthful in the coming week. Use the words *"Sorry I'm late but I didn't leave home early enough."*

Assess Your Progress

At the end of every week, review your progress with your buddy / therapist. Did you mostly arrive late, on time or early? What happened when you arrived early for an event? Did anyone make a comment? Did you get any insights into people's perceptions of your tardiness? Did anyone assume they were late because they arrived after you? Did you have a conversation with someone that you wouldn't have had otherwise? How did being early make you feel?

If you have found this set of activities too hard, and you haven't made any progress, then this in itself is a useful result. Now is the time to consider whether you WANT to improve your time-keeping. Can you think of a reason why you might not be prepared to give up this habit? What rewards does it give you? What are you afraid you might lose from your life? Do you need to seek help, or are you happy to accept this side of yourself? The choice is yours.

FINAL THOUGHTS

We bend time – it's not linear for us. The classic time-management systems don't work for us – in fact, they have the opposite effect. We never want to do the things we SHOULD be doing. When we don't have a deadline, we dither. We never get a job finished early. On the other hand, when we DO have a deadline, and it is getting too close for comfort, we focus on the task and get it done with great efficiency.

Because we can speed up when we need to, the same task can take a very different amount of time. For this reason, we're not good at measuring how long a task will take. We're more likely to underestimate how much time we need to do something. This means that we're not good at planning our own schedules. Dithering can be put to good use, as it makes otherwise unattractive jobs interesting, and we can turn this to our advantage.

Deadlines are important tools to help us get things done, but we can't fool ourselves – they must be external and real. Our partners have an important role to play in helping us manage time, by giving us external deadlines. This isn't an easy role for them to play.

Our life and career choices can help us manage the less comfortable aspects of Timebending, and use our special gifts to their best advantage.

Apart from reminding you what you have learned in this book, these words also serve another purpose. Since Timebenders don't like finishing things, you might never quite get around to reading the last page, so this way, you haven't missed anything if you don't read it.

Good luck with your Timebending, and remember – you're not alone!

APPENDIX

The Myers Briggs Type Indicator

The Myers Briggs Type Indicator (MBTI) is a widely used personality test which divides the population into 16 types, based of four sets of complementary opposites:

Introversion – Extraversion: Our source of personal energy.

Do we draw our energy from our inner world of reflection and ideas (Introverted); or from the external world of people and activities (Extraverted)?

Sensing – Intuition: How we gather our information about the world.

Are we practical, applied and literal (Sensing); or abstract, symbolic and conceptual (Intuitive)?

Thinking – Feeling: How we make our judgements.

Do we come to conclusions in a logical and objective way (Thinking); or in a value-oriented way (Feeling)?

Judging – Perceiving: How much structure and control we need.

Do we prefer to live a planned and organized life, and have a need to conform (Judging); or do we have a preference for spontaneous, flexible living, dislike of routines and authority, and a more rebellious and entrepreneurial spirit (Perceiving)?

The theoretical basis of this book is the Judging – Perceiving function of the MBTI. Isabel Myers (the daughter of Katharine Briggs) developed the rationale for creating the J–P scale for her questionnaire from her interpretation of Jung's comments, in his seminal book Psychological Types, about the direction and purpose of the auxiliary function. She said that a person preferring Perceiving would tend to live "*in a flexible, spontaneous way, aiming to understand life and adapt to it.*" A person preferring Judging will tend to "*live life in a planned, orderly way, aiming to regulate life and control it.*" Isabel Myers said "*Perception without judgment leads to procrastination. Judgment without perception leads to prejudice.*"

The MBTI Manual – A Guide to the Development and Use of the Myers-Briggs Type Indicator, defines the P function as follows: "*People who live in the Perceiving Attitude seem in their outer behavior to be spontaneous, curious, adaptable, and open to what is new and changeable. Their aim is to receive information as long as possible in an effort to miss nothing that might be important.*"

The J-P distribution in the global sample (2018) is 48% – 52%. There is virtually no difference between men and women.

The strength of type preference is one of the strongest influences on the dominance of type behavior, but with this proviso, types which are most likely to have problems with timeliness are ESFP; ISFP; ESTP; ENFP; ENTP; INTP. Together these make up 36% of the global sample.

Jung believed that differences in behavior are innate, and quoted research into twins to demonstrate this. Consequently, Bouchard and Hur (1998) confirmed the genetic influences on personality for the four MBTI scales through their research on twins – 61 identical twins reared apart and 49 non-identical twins reared apart. This is the only behavior genetics study that has examined the MBTI preference scales, but there is extensive research into behavioral genetics which supports the idea that behavioral traits are inherited (e.g., Bouchard, & Loehlin, 2001; Clark & Watson, 2008; Krueger & Johnson, 2008). The facts are considered so reliable that they now have the status of "Law."

- o First Law: All human behavioral traits are heritable.

- o Second Law: The effect of being raised in the same family is smaller than the effect of genes.

- o Third Law: A substantial portion of the variation in complex human behavioral traits is not accounted for by the effects of genes or families. (Turkheimer 2000, p. 160)

The MBTI should be used as a self-development tool, rather than an objective measurement scale, because it is about preference. People are not bound by their genes – they can change their behavior, if they have exterior factors which cause them to do so. This therefore means that people can change their attitude to punctuality. For example, someone with a P preference who has had a parent who is always late, may grow up very focused on being punctual, if lateness has had a negative impact in their childhood. However, the longer the time since they left home, the more they may revert to their natural preference and slide into unpunctuality. Alternatively, someone with a P preference who has always been tardy, may choose to change their behavior if they work in a job which requires timeliness – teaching, for example – but may revert back to type when they retire.

Bibliography and Sources

Bartky, Ian R. (2000), Selling the True Time: Nineteenth-century Timekeeping in America

Business Wire (1998), Paucity of Punctuality Costs Americans Over $3 Billion a Year

Covey, Stephen (1999), 7 Habits of Highly Effective People

Delonzor, Diana (2002), Never Be Late Again: 7 Cures for the Punctually Challenged

Ferrari, Joseph (2010), Psychology of Procrastination: Why People Put Off Important Tasks Until the Last Minute – American Psychological Association

Ferrari Joseph R. Tice Dianne M. (March 2000), Procrastination as a Self-Handicap for Men and Women: A Task-Avoidance Strategy in a Laboratory Setting – Journal of Research in Personality

Fitzsimmons, Sharon Ph.D. (1999), Type and Time Management – Psychometrics Canada Ltd

Garfield, Simon (2016), Timekeepers

Geyer, Peter. (2013), J–P: What is it, really? How it came about, what it means, what it contains, its interpretation and use.

Jaffe, Eric (2013), Why Wait? The Science Behind Procrastination

Kanigel, Robert (1997), The One Best Way: Frederick Winslow Taylor and the Enigma of Efficiency

Levine, Robert V. (1999), The Pace of Life in 31 Countries – Journal of Cross-Cultural Psychology

Myers, Isabel Briggs & McCaulley, M., Quenk, N., & Hammer, A. Manual (1998), A Guide to the Development and Use of the Myers-Briggs Type Indicator

Myers, Isabel Briggs, & Myers, Peter (1980), Gifts Differing

Myers, Isabel Briggs, with revisions by Myers, K. & Kirby, L. (1993), Introduction to Type

Peacock, S.Y. (1995), The timely completion of the dissertation among graduates of five Ph.D. programs at Saint Louis University: The relationships among psychological type, life experiences, support group participation, and perceptions of advisor/advisee relationships.

Pearman, Roger, & Albritton, Sarah. (1997), I'm Not Crazy, I'm Just Not You

Reynierse, James H. (2012), Toward an empirically sound and radically revised type theory – Journal of Psychological Type

Rooney, David (2008), Ruth Belville, The Greenwich Time Lady

Seligman, Martin (2007), What You Can Change and What You Can't

Stewart-Sicking, Joseph A. (2015), Cognitive Therapy and the Punctual Self

Underwood, Lamar (2018), Civil War Stories

Urban, Tim (July 7, 2015), Why I'm Always Late – WaitButWhy.com

YouGov Omnibus Survey (Nov 20, 2014), RealTime Research: Retail & consumer

Acknowledgements

This book would never have been published without my mentor and "deadline buddy" Wendy Berliner, who not only gave me valuable guidance, but heroically helped me to overcome my closure anxiety to get this book finished. Joy Wodziak and Gerry Wright both gave me a valuable push in the right direction. Karen Tweed's complete understanding of Timebending meant that she was able to exceed my expectations with her cartoons. John Campbell's forensic but sympathetic editing made a real difference to the finished book. Simon Deard's proofreading skills were much appreciated.

Rosalind Bubb's sensitive EFT skills set me on the road to self-discovery, and Sue Beer and Emma Roberts helped me on my way. Sarah Veness thoughtfully facilitated my meeting with Dr Alison Baverstock, whose positive reaction helped me to believe this book was worth publishing. My thanks also go to the members of the British Association of Psychological Type, and its international counterpart, the APTi, who have provided me with a platform to test out my theories.

Finally, I'd like to thank the great team of Beta Readers whose input helped to improve each draft of the book: Andy Hunter; Brent Fielder; Clare Rayner; Denise Clarke; Harriet Campbell; Heather Campbell; Jennifer Millman; Mike Sullivan; Richard Moon; Rima Greenhill; Sarah Veness and Val James.

Message from the Author

Thank you for reading my book. It's taken me five years to research and another five years to write, so I'm really hoping you have found these ideas helpful. This is the book I longed to find, to help me with my lateness habit, but because it didn't exist, I decided to write it myself.

If you have found it insightful, would you help me pass on the message by leaving me a review online? Without reviews, all my efforts are likely to sink without trace – just a few words will really help.

Not everyone realizes that I struggle to be on time, so I'm a bit crazy to go public and admit the mental hoops I jump through to avoid being late. I've decided to write this book because, whenever I've shared my ideas with other people who have the same problem, they always want to know more, but can't seem to find any other information on the subject.

In spite of my struggles with time I've somehow managed to turn up for enough classes to gain a B.A. and a Master's Degree. I've worked through the midnight hours as a business consultant, I've researched hundreds of markets to understand how people around the world make their buying decisions, and I've just made it to meetings in time to help major global businesses redesign their strategic marketing. I've squeezed in qualifications in Myers Briggs, Neuro-Linguistic Programming, Emotional Freedom Technique, Hypnotherapy, and Marketing.

In between, I've worked out my ideas for this book, searched out and interviewed people who are struggling with punctuality, and reviewed all the research I could find on the subject. I've been distracted by Facebook and Twitter, and even wrote and published another book, as a double bind. Eventually I've managed to apply everything I've learned to my own behavior, and overcome my closure anxiety, in order to get this manuscript finished. I hope it will help some of the other Timebenders out there to accept that there are aspects of their lives which they can't always control; to acknowledge the impact their behavior has on others; to recognize that in certain areas they have special strengths; and to improve their own relationship with time.

Keep in Contact

I hope you found this book helpful but a book is only a start. If you want to find supportive buddies online, then check these out.

- o Website: www.timebending.co.uk
- o Facebook page: Not Late but Timebending
- o Facebook group: Not Late but Timebending group
- o Twitter: @OnlyTimebending

Lightning Source UK Ltd.
Milton Keynes UK
UKHW011155141020
371568UK00001B/132

9 781838 070519